A Brief History of New Mexico

by

Myra Ellen Jenkins

Albert H. Schroeder

Published for the
CULTURAL PROPERTIES REVIEW COMMITTEE
in cooperation with the State Planning Office

by
THE UNIVERSITY OF NEW MEXICO PRESS
Albuquerque   1974

This publication is funded through the special revolving fund
appropriated by the 31st New Mexico State Legislature.

D0176247

An official publication of the Cultural Properties Review Committee of the State of New Mexico by the University of New Mexico Press. All rights reserved. Library of Congress Catalog Card Number 74-21917. International Standard Book Number 0-8263-0370-6. Manufactured in the United States of America. First edition

PREFACE

This short history is reprinted from a portion of Volume I of the two-volume *The Historic Preservation Program for New Mexico,* published in 1973 by the State Planning Office, and includes many of the illustrations which appeared in Volume II of that study. *The Historic Preservation Program for New Mexico* detailed the results of five years of concerted action on the part of the New Mexico professional Cultural Properties Review Committee, in cooperation with the State Planning Office and with the assistance of local historical and archeological organizations and other interested persons, to fulfill New Mexico's obligations in carrying out the intent of the Cultural Properties Act passed by the 1969 state legislature and the National Historic Preservation Act of 1966. It is hoped that this account will be of use to students and teachers of New Mexico history as well as of interest to historically-minded citizens and especially to out-of-state visitors at state parks and monuments.

The selected bibliography makes no pretense of being comprehensive and is intended only as a guide to the reader. It includes some readily available general sources, a few firsthand accounts concerning aspects of certain themes and representative specialized scholarly studies. The latter should be consulted for more extensive bibliographies within the scope of their concentration. Professional journals also contain in-depth articles dealing with particular periods, events, developments and interpretations.

This narrative attempts to interpret the story of New Mexico within the framework of several themes which the Cultural Properties Review Committee felt ran throughout the state's unique tricultural history: (1) the original inhabitants; (2) exploration and settlement; (3) westward expansion; (4) political and military affairs; (5) commerce and trade; (6) ranching and agriculture; (7) lumbering and mining; (8) science and engineering; (9) architecture; (10) religion, culture and education.

The authors express their indebtedness to the following fellow members of the professional Cultural Properties Review Committee who helped develop the thematic structure and provided guidance and editorial assistance in the preparation of this brief study: Historians Marc Simmons and Spencer Wilson; Architects John P. Conron and George Clayton Pearl, Archeologist George H. Ewing and Governor's Special Advisor E. Boyd. Credit is also due to State Planning Officer David W. King, who also serves as State Historic Preservation Officer, and his staff, particularly to Planner Daniel E. Reiley, for their consistent support of the entire historic preservation program. Acknowedgment for constant service is also made to James H. Purdy, staff member of the State Records Center and Archives.

Myra Ellen Jenkins

Albert H. Schroeder

Santa Fe, New Mexico, 1974

CONTENTS

ILLUSTRATIONS

New Mexico holds a unique tricultural position in the history of the United States. Most of the villages of the modern Pueblo Indians are still located on or near the same sites as when first seen by the Spaniards in the middle of the sixteenth century. The archeological remains of others, long since abandoned, are still identifiable as are the habitations of the nomadic tribes of Apaches, Navajos and Comanches who entered New Mexico after the conquest. Since its construction in 1610 as headquarters for the Villa of Santa Fe, the flags of four sovereignties have flown over the adobe Palace of the Governors, the oldest public building in the United States, including the royal ensign of Spain, the proud eagle of the Mexican Republic, the flag of the United States of America and, for a few days in 1862, the Confederate stars and bars. For the brief period of 1680–1693 the venerable building was also headquarters for the victorious Indians during the great Pueblo Revolt. Today, in New Mexico, descendants of all ethnic groups represented throughout its long history still live, work, create, vote and hold office.

7th Century Pit House
E. T. Hall, Jr.

Original Inhabitants

The known prehistory of New Mexico ranges from about 12,000 B.C., or earlier, to A.D. 1540. During the earliest period, man in the Southwest hunted big game, such as mammoth, and lived in the open or in cave shelters. Sandia Cave, the earliest known archeological site in the Southwest, and the Folsom Site, where man's association with extinct fauna was first definitely demonstrated in the Southwest, are the two which have received national attention in the scientific field, along with later investigations at the Clovis Site near Anderson Basin.

As the large animals died off during the last phase of the ice age, about 8,000 B.C., the Southwestern hunter turned to smaller game and placed more emphasis on gathering wild foods. Toward the latter part of this Archaic Period, about 3,000 B.C., he also adopted the idea of agriculture from neighbors in Mexico. Bat Cave on the San Agustin Plains of western New Mexico has yielded the earliest domestic maize to date. Though this farming probably was marginal at best, it restricted the hunting and gathering cycle to smaller areas so that the people could return to plant and harvest their crops at the appropriate time of the year. Also during this period, cultural differences developed to distinguish the more southern nomads within the state, the Cochise, from the San José in the northwestern part.

As these people came to depend more and more on their small farms, they became more sedentary in their ways and adopted

1

Pueblo of Jémez

ideas such as making pottery from neighbors in Mexico and Arizona. Pit houses for year-round residence and communal ceremonial structures forced the Indians living in small permanent villages to trade for items they had previously picked up while on wide-ranging, hunting and gathering parties. Architectural and ceramic decoration, as well as other aspects of the material culture of the time, developed into different regional styles. The early sedentary developments in southern and western New Mexico became known as the Mogollon Culture (pit house, brown and red pottery, and large community ceremonial lodge) and those in the north as the Anasazi (pit house, gray pottery, and small extended family ceremonial lodge).

The Mogollon, the first group to make pottery in New Mexico, influenced the people of northern New Mexico and by A.D. 200 or 300 had introduced the idea of pottery and village life to them. By the A.D. 500's, the Anasazi pattern of living grew out of these contacts and expanded throughout the Four Corners region.

These small villages of probably kin-related, sedentary farming people maintained inter-community contacts, surface-mined hematite and turquoise, quarried chert and obsidian as well as stone slabs for constructing walls, and traded for items not available locally such as shell from the Pacific Coast. The Mogollon of southwestern New Mexico gradually developed larger villages such as Woodrow Ruin, Gila Cliff Dwellings, and Kwil-

2

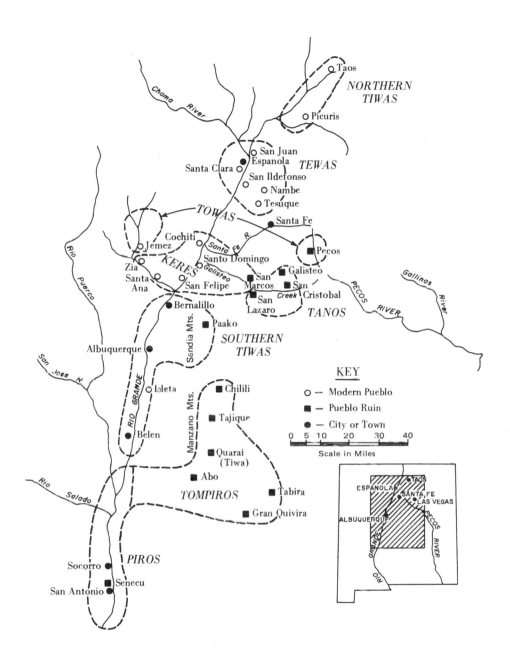

New Mexico Pueblo Linguistic Groups
Albert H. Schroeder

Pecos National Monument
National Park Service

leylekia Ruin which are surface dwellings. The material culture exhibited by these sites differs from one another because of time difference and influences from neighboring groups. Farther north, in west-central New Mexico, pueblos such as Apache Creek Ruin show a mixture of Mogollon and Anasazi ideas.

In the 1000's the Anasazi living in northwestern New Mexico began to surpass the Mogollon in architectural accomplishments and in the development of large communities. The Anasazi of the Manuelito area, Chaco Canyon and Aztec Ruins National Monuments, along with the nearby Salmon Ruins, developed multistoried pueblos enclosing a large plaza which contained a sizeable circular, ceremonial structure. About the same time, these people began using water control devices to irrigate their fields. They also developed a complex of roads, particularly those leading out of Chaco Canyon in a number of directions. Their towns represent the highest developments achieved in New Mexico on the west side of the Continental Divide prior to A.D. 1300. Several areas in this part of New Mexico contain a series of sites representing different periods of occupation covering as much as 600 to 700 years, such as Two Grey Hills and the Skunk Springs Archeological Districts.

East of the divide, the Anasazi in the north-central Rio Grande drainage area received ideas from the west via the San José drainage as early as the 600 to 700's. However, when they adopted surface architecture several hundred years later, they mostly built single story houses of mud or of mud and wood. Not until a great drought in the late 1200's forced many of the Indians on the west side of the divide to abandon their farms and move east into the Rio Grande Valley did the pueblos of north-central New Mexico develop into larger communities, as seen at Bandelier National Monument, Castle on the Chama, Tsiping, and other ruins.

Though development along the Rio Grande Valley prior to A.D. 1300 had not been of particular consequence, that to the east of the valley was even less. Contingents of Mogollon and Anasazi families drifted across the valley, between A.D. 700 and 900, into the southeastern and northeastern parts of the state respectively, settling in small farming villages east of the mountains, like The Three Rivers Petroglyph and Pueblo Site.

By A.D. 1300, however, these groups had either joined relatives along the Rio Grande or concentrated in a few favorable areas east of the mountains, such as Pecos and the Gran Quivira National

5

Collection of Pottery at the Museum of New Mexico

Pueblo of Taos
New Mexico Department of Development

Monument area. These frontier pueblos became trading centers for Plains Indians. After the drought of the late 1200's west of the divide, a few pueblos survived in the Zuni area, like Heshotauthla and Yellow House Ruin, and a few near Luna, New Mexico. Those who migrated east to the Rio Grande at this time introduced new ideas, including glaze-paint decorated pottery.

As a result of these population shifts, most of the major pueblos which survived into historic times got their start, including Hawikuh, the first pueblo contacted by the Spaniards, as well as Kiakima, Kwakima, Kechepewan, Matsaki and other Zuni-speaking pueblos. Ácoma to the east, as well as other existing Keres-speaking pueblos, along with the Tiwa towns from Taos Pueblo on the north to Isleta on the south with the Tewa pueblos between them, had their beginnings in the 1300's. The Piro pueblos in the Socorro area and the Tompiro pueblos in the present Mountainair region, such as Abó and Pueblo Colorado, also became major centers at this time as did Galisteo Pueblo, Pueblo of San Lázaro, and other Tano sites in the Galisteo Basin area and the Towa pueblos of Jémez.

7

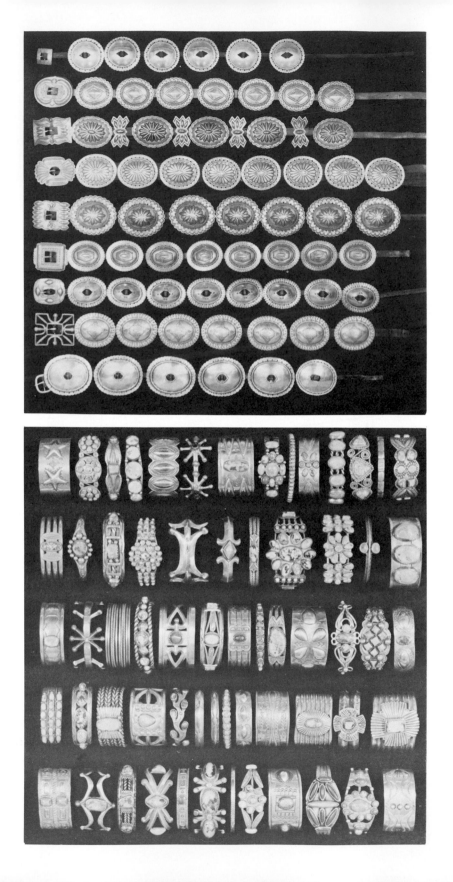

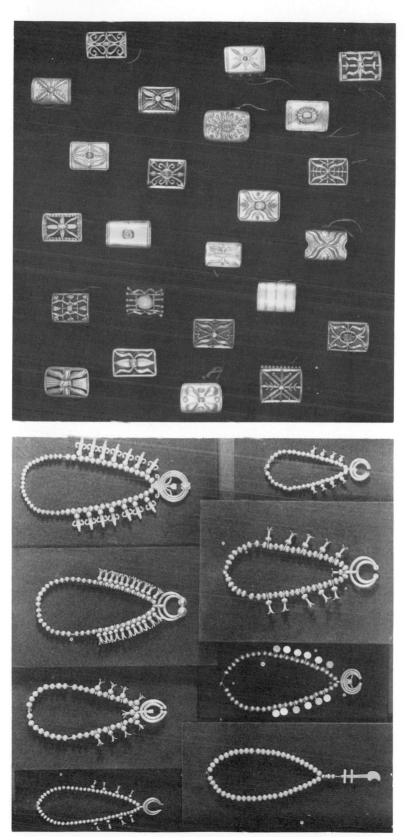

Collection of Indian Jewelry,
Museum of New Mexico

Each of these individual pueblos, or in some cases language groups, had developed their individual styles of pottery making. Some pueblos had economic advantages, such as the Keres of San Marcos Pueblo and possibly others with the turquoise mines in Cerrillos Hills, the Jémez with their obsidian deposits, or the Tompiros with the salt deposits in the lakes east of their pueblos. All farms directly alongside the Rio Grande, as well as those on tributary streams, were watered by irrigation canals. Other pueblos away from live streams, dependent on rainfall for their crops, suffered heavily from a drought in the late 1500's.

This latter situation led to the abandonment of the Pajarito Plateau, on which Bandelier National Monument and Puyé are located, and of the Chama drainage where large sites like Sapawe were occupied. All occupation on tributary streams seems to have been affected, including the Jémez area. Others living off the mainstream, such as the Tompiros, managed to survive for about another 100 years.

By the time of Spanish entry in 1540, most of the pueblos of New Mexico had adopted a square to rectangular ground plan with a central plaza surrounded by multi-storied dwellings terraced back from the plaza. Taos Pueblo, with two compact units separated by a plaza, is and was the most famous exception. Individual houses in each varied from three to ten or more rooms per family, depending on the number of stories in the pueblo. The ground level rooms normally had no openings, entry to the pueblo being by exterior ladders to the top of the first story, and others above. Turkey pens, a variety of dogs, and nearby farmlands were common to most pueblos. The only major change in the pueblos brought about by the Spaniards was the addition of a mission church and convento as at Giusewa and other sites occupied at the time of Spanish settlement. Laguna Pueblo, however, was not officially established until the late 1690's, a direct result of the Pueblo Rebellion of 1680–92, which also led to the establishment and brief occupation of Kotyiti Pueblo.

The Apaches, entering the Southwest from the plains, possibly in the early to middle 1500's, had established friendly relations with the eastern pueblos by the time of Spanish arrival, though some friction might have developed with the Piros on the south. After Spanish settlement, different names were applied to Apache groups, including the Navajos. Friction between the Navajos and

Utes in the early 1700's led to the Navajos building crude masonry sites in which to take refuge, as at Crow Canyon District, or to concentrate in small villages away from the Utes, as on Big Bead Mesa.

New Mexico is fortunate that the direct descendants of the late prehistoric groups have for the most part survived to the present day. Their contributions to the cultural mixture which developed in the state have provided a unique heritage. The pueblos still remain as viable centers with their own identity, language and customs.

1784 Spanish Coin Found at Pecos National Monument
National Park Service

New Mexico Under Spain

Exploration and Conquest

A shipwreck, persistent rumors of gold and legends of great Indian civilizations were responsible for the first European exploration of New Mexico. In the spring of 1536, four ragged travelers, Alvar Nuñez Cabeza de Vaca, Alonzo de Castillo Maldonado, Andrés Dorantes and his Moorish slave, Estevan, arrived at the city of Culiacán, Mexico. They were the sole survivors of the ill-fated Narvaez expedition which had been shipwrecked near present Galveston, Texas in 1528, and after five years of Indian captivity had escaped and made their way by foot from the Gulf of Mexico through western Texas, northern Mexico and halfway down the west coast. Along the way they had heard tales from local Indians of great riches to be found in the "Seven Cities of Cíbola" inhabited by highly civilized tribes to the north which they repeated to a credulous audience. Soon they were in Mexico City, capital of the Viceroyalty of New Spain, telling their stories to Viceroy Antonio de Mendoza who became enthusiastic about the possibility of adding further wealth and fame to his own position.

Mendoza was unwilling, however, to risk a large expedition to the north without further confirmation, and in 1539 the Franciscan friar, Marcos de Niza, led a reconnaissance party from Culiacán, with Estevan as guide, northward through present Arizona. The advance party of Estevan entered the village of Hawikuh, discovering instead of "seven gold cities" a number of multistoried villages of the Zuni Pueblo Indians. Estevan was killed, but several of his party escaped to carry the word of the disaster to Marcos de Niza who retreated to Mexico.

Attempting to turn defeat into partial victory, however, the

Franciscan told even more extravagant stories about possible wealth to the north. As a result, aristocratic young Francisco Vásques de Coronado, governor of Nueva Galicia, led his ill-fated expedition of 300 soldiers and 800 Indians from Compostela to Hawikuh in 1540. Great was his disappointment on reaching the Zuni pueblos to find that there were no golden cities, only agricultural communities who had no intention of submitting to the invaders but instead attacked them, killing several soldiers and wounding Coronado before being defeated by the superior arms of the Spaniards.

After capturing the Zuni villages, Coronado sent out various expeditions. García López de Cardenas went west to discover the Grand Canyon. Pedro de Tovar found the seven villages of the Hopis who also resisted, a practice of these western pueblos which they continued to follow throughout the Spanish period.

In August 1540, Hernando de Alvarado, led by the Indian "Bigotes" who had come to Hawikuh from the eastern pueblo of Cicuyé (Pecos), went eastward into the province of the Tiwa Indians in the Rio Grande valley known as *Tiguex*, visiting the Pueblo of Ácoma high on its protected rock along the way. From a stopping place near present Bernalillo he sent word back to Coronado that he had found an excellent site for winter headquarters. Accompanied by Bigotes, Alvarado ascended the Rio Grande visiting the northern pueblos as far as Taos. After returning briefly to Tiguex, the party set forth for Pecos, turning east along the Galisteo River into the land of the Tanos and after crossing the mountains at present Glorieta Pass reached the imposing multi-storied Pueblo of Pecos, gateway to the vast eastern buffalo plains. At Pecos, Alvarado met another guide, probably of Plains Indian rather than of Pueblo stock, whom he dubbed "El Turco" (the Turk) because of his facial features. El Turco, anxious to lure the Spaniards away from the pueblos, convinced Alvarado that the area of great wealth, referred to as "Quivira," did indeed exist, but far to the northeast. After a brief reconnaissance trip east from Pecos, Alvarado and his Indian guides returned to Tiguex where Coronado and the main body of troops had moved into winter headquarters at the recommended site.

It was a hard winter. When food and supplies ran short, the Spanish took what they wanted from the thus far friendly Indians who rebelled. After a siege of seven weeks, the natives were defeated, but bitterness towards the intruders remained.

14

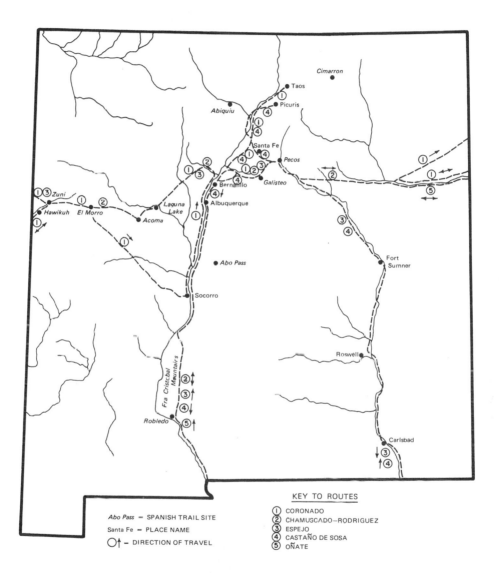

Cimarron

Taos
Abiquiu ①④ Picuris
①
④
Santa Fe
④① ④ Pecos ① →
② ③ ④ ③ ② →
① ③ Bernalillo ① ② Galisteo ② ①
② ④ ⑤ ←
① ③ Zuni ① ② ④ ③
Hawikuh El Morro Laguna Albuquerque ③
① Lake ① ④
Acoma ①
① Abo Pass Fort
Sumner
Socorro

Roswell

②
③ Fra Cristobal Mountains
④
Robledo ⑤
Carlsbad
③
④

KEY TO ROUTES
Abo Pass = SPANISH TRAIL SITE   ① CORONADO
Santa Fe = PLACE NAME   ② CHAMUSCADO–RODRIGUEZ
◯↑ = DIRECTION OF TRAVEL   ③ ESPEJO
                                      ④ CASTAÑO DE SOSA
                                      ⑤ OÑATE

Major Spanish Exploration Routes in New Mexico
Albert H. Schroeder

Inscription by Juan de Oñate at El Morro National Monument
New Mexico Department of Development

Palace of the Governors, Santa Fe
Karl Kernberger

In the spring of 1541 Coronado and his men proceeded to Pecos, then set out for the place called Quivira, led by El Turco, while another detachment was sent from Tiguex up the Rio Grande as far as Taos to confiscate supplies from the northern pueblos. On their exhausting 77-day trip, the Spaniards penetrated deeply into the plains of Kansas, but found only the straw encampments of a few Plains Indians. Convinced that El Turco had lured them there to massacre them, the Spaniards killed their guide and returned at once to Tiguex, where the situation deteriorated still further, and mutterings of mutiny were heard. Coronado retreated to Mexico in April 1542, leaving behind the Franciscan Juan de Padilla and two lay brothers. All were later killed by the Indians.

For nearly forty years the New Mexico project was abandoned by the authorities in Mexico City. In 1581 Fray Agustín Rodríguez and two other Franciscans, in company with a small detachment of soldiers under Captain Francisco Chamuscado, came up the Rio Grande, fording the river near present El Paso. They followed the east bank of the river as far as present Rincon before striking off through the dreaded 100-mile *jornada del muerto* (journey of the dead man) east of the San Cristobal mountains. After leaving the desert, the expedition crossed the river south of Socorro and continued north along the west bank into the region traversed by Coronado The route which they blazed soon became the *camino real* which would be followed by colonists, soldiers, supply and commercial caravans for the next three centuries.

The Rodríguez-Chamuscado expedition explored the area from Zuni to the buffalo plains east of the Pecos River and the Galisteo Basin. The friars remained to suffer martyrdom, but the soldiers returned to Mexico. The next year (1582), Antonio de Espejo and Fray Bernaldino Beltrán led another expedition to determine the fate of the priests. At Puaray, in Tiguex, they learned that the priests had been killed, and after a brief exploration trip, they returned to Mexico by way of the Pecos River.

Two other ill-fated and unauthorized expeditions entered New Mexico. In 1590, Gaspar Castaño de Sosa led an exploration party to Pecos and the villages of the upper Rio Grande as far north as Picurís, but was arrested by representatives of the viceroy and returned to Mexico to face charges of leading an unauthorized expedition. A few years later, Captain Francisco Leyva de Bonilla and Juan de Humaña also penetrated western Kansas. The two leaders quarrelled and Bonilla was killed. Indians then massacred

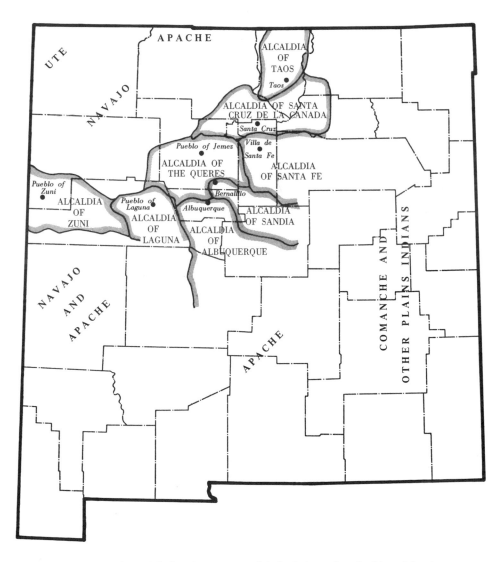

Spanish Settlement and Administration in New Mexico
J. Richard Salazar

the rest of Humaña's party. In 1595 wealthy Juan de Oñate of Zacatecas received a contract from the Spanish Crown to colonize the northern frontier of New Mexico.

During the more than half-century which elapsed between European penetration in 1539 and permanent settlement, the Indian world shrank still further so that many pueblos in existence when Estevan arrived at Hawikuh were abandoned. Archeological evidence indicates that continued drought was again the major factor and probably accounted for the desertion of several Rio Grande villages in the Bandelier Monument area and along the Chama tributary. Groups from these areas settled among their relatives in the pueblos located along the Rio Grande.

Early Settlement

On January 8, 1598, Oñate led his expedition of ten Franciscans and 129 soldier-colonists, many of them with their families, out of San Bartolomé. With them came the poet-soldier Gaspar Pérez de Villagrá to record the epic of their exploits in his "Historia del Nuevo Méjico." In addition to the necessary military supplies, the colonists brought their household effects, domestic livestock and seeds and shrubs to be planted in their new homes. Entering New Mexico at the El Paso crossing, the expedition followed the Espejo route into the Rio Grande valley meeting no opposition from the Indians. By July 11, they had reached the Indian village of Ohke on the east bank of the Rio Grande, which they renamed "San Juan de los Caballeros," where Oñate established temporary camp. Within a few months, however, he moved his headquarters across the Rio Grande to the village of Yuqueyunque, and founded the first European settlement of San Gabriel.

The pueblo leaders voluntarily took oaths of allegiance to the Spanish Crown required by Oñate, although they undoubtedly did not understand the meaning of becoming royal vassals, and accepted the ministrations of the Franciscans assigned to each pueblo.

Oñate's conquest of New Mexico was completed in 1599 after his soldiers stormed the rebellious Pueblo of Ácoma. Events at San Gabriel, however, did not go well; the first winter was harsh and many colonists abandoned the little settlement. The few loyal followers were later joined by others from Mexico. Oñate led several expeditions in the years that followed, one to the mouth of the Colorado River in 1605. On his return trip he camped at the water hole at the foot of El Morro and cut his name on the famous Inscription Rock between Zuni and Ácoma, becoming the first of thousands of white travelers to leave their signatures and messages on that great sandstone landmark where Indians for centuries had also carved their petroglyphs.

The difficulties of early settlement and complaints of the colonists caused Oñate to fall into official disfavor. In 1608 he was succeeded as governor by Pedro de Peralta who located the capital at Santa Fe in 1610. The traditional Spanish plaza was laid out in the center of the new *villa* and the massive Palace of the Governors was built to serve as the administrative headquarters. Santa Fe is still the capital of New Mexico, and the plaza, reduced somewhat in size, and the Palace of the Governors are still the center of the city.

From 1610 to 1680 other colonists moved into New Mexico and established haciendas and settlements all along the Rio Grande and its tributaries from the Socorro region to the Taos valley. Priests of the Franciscan Order of Friars Minor, to whom the religious affairs of New Mexico were assigned, introduced stock raising and new crafts to the pueblos under their ministrations and supervised the building of imposing mission churches, teaching the Indians new methods of utilizing sun-dried adobe bricks and stone construction.

Events were, however, far from peaceful. Civil and religious authorities quarrelled constantly over which one had superior authority. Intrigue among the settlers was rife. In spite of the laws guaranteeing their just treatment as royal vassals, the Pueblos were often mistreated. Illegal exactions were made upon them and they were particularly resentful over attempts to suppress their native religious rites so that by late in the century conditions were ripe for revolt. Various cultural factors had also contributed to further abandonment of many pueblos. Increasing numbers of plains Apaches migrated into New Mexico from the east and by the 1640's, these nomads had become skillful horsemen. Steadfastly refusing to accept white rule, they successfully raided the outlying Spanish settlements, attacked the Galisteo pueblos and decimated the Piro and Tompiro villages east of the Rio Grande valley. Even the great stone missions of Quarai, Abó and Gran Quivira were deserted by 1680.

20

*Stone Reredos of Our Lady of Light in the Church of
Cristo Rey, Santa Fe
Richard Federici*

The Pueblo Revolt

Under the leadership of Popé, a San Juan Indian living at Taos, Naranjo and others, the pueblos for the only time in their history united and exploded into revolt in August 1680. Most of the settlers and Franciscans in the outlying areas were massacred. Those who escaped fled into Santa Fe or concentrated in the present Albuquerque area. The rebels laid seige to the Palace of the Governors within whose walls the surviving northern colonists gathered. Lack of water and provisions forced the Spanish, led by wounded Governor Otermín, to retreat southward, taking with them only the barest of necessities and the small wooden image of Our Lady of the Assumption, their most revered religious saint which had originally been brought to New Mexico in 1625. Simultaneously, the surviving settlers in the *Rio Abajo* (lower river) had also begun their retreat, accompanied by some loyal Piro allies from the pueblos of Alamillo, Senecú and Socorro and some Tiwas from Isleta. The two parties joined forces near present El Paso and crossed the river where Otermín established his headquarters close to the Manso Indian mission of Our Lady of Guadalupe. Both he and his successor, Domingo Jironza Petríz de Cruzate attempted to recapture New Mexico, but to no avail.

Indian governors ruled New Mexico for the next twelve years from headquarters which they, too, established in the Palace of the Governors. Popé tried to keep the Indians united, but individual rivalries among various pueblos were too strong, and the leaders soon fought among themselves and with the Apaches who had joined them in the revolt.

Reestablishment of Spanish Control

In 1691 Captain General Diego de Vargas Zapata Lujan Ponce de León y Contreras succeeded Cruzate as governor of New Mexico and immediately began plans for a systematic reconquest of the area for the Crown. His small army left El Paso in late August 1692, marched up the Rio Grande, accepting the submission of the pueblos along the way, and by September 14 was in possession of Santa Fe and the Palace of the Governors, without having fought a single battle.

After securing the submission of the northern pueblos, de Vargas and his soldiers turned westward to complete the pacification as far as the Hopi villages and returned to El Paso. He had succeeded in a bloodless reoccupation of New Mexico within four months. In 1693 he returned with a larger group of colonists and Franciscans to resettle the vast area, but the Indian leaders in Santa Fe, remembering past troubles, gave battle. The Spaniards quickly recaptured Santa Fe, attributing their success partially to the presence of the statue of Our Lady of the Assumption which they had brought back with them and who now acquired the title of "La Conquistadora." Although Santa Fe was taken, Pueblo resistance was not completely broken until 1696.

From the reconquest by de Vargas until 1821, New Mexico remained the northern frontier outpost of the Viceroyalty of New Spain. The colonists who returned with de Vargas were soon joined by an increasing number of new settlers. To provide for the expanding population a formal land grant system developed by which the governors in a clearly defined procedure made grants from the royal domain to both individual Spaniards and to groups of family heads who established separate communities, some of which were fortified to serve as outposts against hostile Indian incursions. In the settlement grants, cultivatable land was divided among the heads of households while the large areas of grazing land were used in common. Acequias were built to irrigate crops grown along the narrow valleys, but stock raising became much more important and the economy was essentially pastoral. This system of land tenure continued through the Mexican period until U.S. occupation in 1846.

In making the grants, however, the governor was to strictly enforce the many provisions of the great law code known as the *Recopilación de Leyes de los Reynos de las Indias* protecting the lands used and occupied by sedentary Indians from white encroachment. Some governors, particularly de Vargas himself, did not always literally obey these laws, but by and large later governors did enforce them and the pueblos quickly learned to take their complaints against trespassers to Santa Fe where decisions were often made in their favor.

In 1695 de Vargas made the first recorded settlement grant for the new Villa of Santa Cruz de la Cañada which then became the administrative center for the area north of Santa Fe throughout the Spanish and early Mexican periods. A few years earlier, the Tano pueblos of San Cristobal and San Lázaro had been forced out of the Galisteo Basin by Apache attacks and had relocated opposite each other on both sides of the Santa Cruz river at the site chosen by de Vargas as the plaza for the new villa. San Lázaro was ordered to resettle at Yuqueyunque and San Cristobal at Chimayó, but both pueblos fled their new locations during the 1696 revolt. In 1706 a third villa was established at Albuquerque to administer the lower area of the Rio Grande.

Further shifts in Indian population took place during the revolt and reconquest. Inter-tribal hostilities while the Spanish were gone caused the Keres pueblos between Santa Fe and the Bernalillo area to take refuge on nearby mesas. With reoccupation, de Vargas persuaded them to return to their former villages. The Zunis, menaced by the Apaches, merged into one village. The Piros and Isletas who had gone with the Spanish to El Paso stayed in that area where land had been given them. Those Isletas who remained in New Mexico as well as the inhabitants of the other Tiwa villages of Sandia, Puaray and Alameda, fled to the Hopis because of attacks by the Keres and Jémez. By 1712 the Isletas had returned from Hopiland and Sandia was reestablished in 1748. The 1696 revolt caused large numbers of Indians to again flee their homes. The Tewa villages of Jacona and Cuyamungue north of Santa Fe, as well as Tano San Lázaro and San Cristobal, were permanently abandoned as their inhabitants fled to the Hopis, although some later returned and integrated into Santa Clara and other permanent Tewa villages. Refugees from Cieneguilla, Santo Domingo, Cochití and Zia fled to Ácoma. The nearby mission of Laguna, formed largely by refugees, was established in 1699. Many Picurís took off for the plains and some from Jémez took refuge in the mountains or with the Navajos, but both groups had returned by 1706.

Throughout the century, epidemics, especially smallpox, periodically took a heavy toll of Pueblo lives and together with continued Apache and Comanche attacks caused the abandonment of the Pueblo of Galisteo in the 1780's and finally of Pecos during the Mexican period.

Campaigns against the Apaches, Navajos, Utes and Comanches who raided both the pueblos and the settlements characterized the entire 18th century. During the 1720's more Apaches moved from the plains into New Mexico and south Texas, and the Comanches took their place as raiders from the east. The Comanches were inveterate traders, however, and by the middle of the century

Las Trampas
National Park Service

Spaniards and Pueblos were exchanging goods with them at annual trade fairs held at the Pueblo of Taos. In spite of this, Comanches often raided the northern haciendas and pueblos. By the 1750's the Utes were attacking the region north of San Juan Pueblo and had forced the Navajos south and west from their homeland so that they came into conflict with the western pueblos of Zuni, Ácoma, Laguna and Jémez. Thus, the Pueblo Indians and the Spanish settlements were virtually surrounded by hostile forces. Had the governors not been able to take advantage of inter-tribal enmity by making temporary alliances with one tribe against another, New Mexico would have been overwhelmed. The Pueblo Indians willingly supplied their share of militia auxiliaries to serve with the Spaniards in campaigns against the nomadic groups.

As a result of these contacts with the hostile tribes a new ethnic strain, the *genízaro*, was added to the New Mexican population. The genízaros were displaced Indians who had lost their original tribal identity through capture, usually as children, by other tribes. They were in turn ransomed or bought by the Spaniards or simply wandered into settled areas. Some became servants or laborers. By the mid-1700's, their numbers were so large that groups of them were given settlement grants at Abiquiu, Belen, Tomé and later at San Miguel. They accepted Christianity, agreed to live in a Europeanized status and often intermarried with the Spaniards.

The governor continued to be responsible directly to the viceroy until 1776. In addition to making the land grants and otherwise providing for the welfare of both Spanish subjects and Pueblo Indians, he was head of the presidial troops and could order the formation of militia. He appointed the chief local officials known as *alcaldes mayores* who administered the eight local *alcaldías*. Municipal government, especially that of the Villa of Santa Fe, was left largely to the *cabildo*, later to village town councils known as *ayuntamientos*.

In spite of the governor's subordination to the viceroy, New Mexico received little support from the capital in Mexico City in the constant military struggle. The viceroy himself was faced with similar problems of vainly attempting to defend the entire northern frontier of Mexico against hostile attacks and it was impossible to send reenforcements to Santa Fe. To consolidate the administration of the borderlands in order to cope with the

El Santuario de Chimayó
Richard Federici

La Conquistadora, Santa Fe
E. Boyd Collection,
State Records Center and Archives

San Estévan de Ácoma Mission Church
Leland H. Marmon

problem, the Spanish Crown in 1776 separated the northern provinces, including New Mexico, from the control of the viceroy and organized them into the *provincias internas* (internal provinces) directly under the control of a military official known as the *Comandante General* with headquarters at Arispe in Sonora and later at Chihuahua. The first governor responsible directly to the Comandante General was Juan Bautista de Anza. His concerted campaigns against the Comanches resulted in the 1779 defeat of their great leader Cuerno Verde and a peace treaty in 1786 which opened up the eastern plains to increased exploration and trade. Navajo and Apache difficulties, however, continued.

With the reconquest, the Franciscan friars returned to the missions and the spiritual administration of both Pueblo Indian and Spaniard. They reestablished abandoned pueblos, repaired the churches which had fallen into ruin during the revolt and supervised the construction of new ones. Unfortunately, the old quarrel of church and state was renewed. As the 18th century progressed, Franciscan influence declined and the Bishop of Durango increasingly asserted his spiritual authority. In 1760 Bishop Pedro Tamarón made an extensive visitation of New Mexico in person and noted in his journal that a large military chapel facing the Santa Fe plaza was being completed and the Governor Marín del Valle and his wife had paid for its construction as well as for the great white stone reredos which was being installed. Today, this reredos, carved by craftsmen brought from Mexico, adorns the huge adobe Church of Cristo Rey in Santa Fe.

In spite of Indian threats and declining numbers, the Franciscans continued their missionary and exploring activities among the non-Christianized tribes, but with little success. In 1775 Fray Sylvestre Vélez de Escalante of Zuni traveled westward to Hopi country in another attempt to convert these Pueblos, who had always resisted Spanish control, and to learn the feasibility of finding a direct route from New Mexico to the recently established California missions. At the same time, Fray Francisco Garcés was attempting to establish a route from California to New Mexico. The following year, Fray Francisco Atanasio Domínguez arrived in Santa Fe with orders from his superiors in Mexico City to make a complete visitation of the missions and also to locate a route to California. On July 29, 1776 Escalante and Domíngez, accompanied by a small military force, set out on a six-month expedition to search for a possible northern route, exploring much of southwestern Colorado and Utah. Although no route to California was completed, the basis for the later Spanish Trail to the coast was laid and much of the Ute country was mapped.

Before leaving on the expedition, Domínguez made his visitation of the missions, and the detailed report which he wrote to his superiors is a graphic description of late 18th century New Mexico.

Franciscan influence continued to decline after the Domínguez visitation as the friars departed or died. Since the Bishop of Durango did not have sufficient seculars to replace them, many churches and chapels were vacant by the end of Spanish rule in 1821.

For more than two hundred years the camino real through Chihuahua was the single trade route of any significance. By the mid-1700's, merchants in Chihuahua, subsidized by the central government, had replaced the earlier supply caravans which had come every three years to provide for the Franciscan missions. Because of the small population, primitive economy and lack of hard money, New Mexican merchants suffered from an unfavorable balance of trade, especially since their risks along the long dangerous route were much higher than those of the Chihuahua merchants.

The Comanches were virtually the only other source of trade. They brought goods from the Mississippi Valley which they had received by trade with the Pawnees into the Taos fairs. After the 1786 Comanche treaty, some Pueblo Indians and poor Hispanic citizens made regular trips to the plains to trade foodstuffs for buffalo meat, hides and occasionally for a horse or mule. This barter *comanchero* trade lasted until stopped by U.S. military campaigns against the Comanches in the late 1800's.

The colonial policy of forbidding foreigners to enter Spanish lands was the chief deterrent to trade. A few Frenchmen, such as the Mallet brothers in 1739, however, came into New Mexico from the east. After the transfer of Louisiana to Spain from France, an attempt was made by Pedro Vial in 1792 to explore an overland route between Santa Fe and St. Louis, but before a trail could be developed, Louisiana was returned to France in 1800, sold to the United States three years later, and the old exclusion policy was again in force. When Zebulon Pike entered New Mexico territory on his exploration of the extent of the Louisiana Purchase in 1806, he was taken prisoner and sent in chains to Chihuahua. Other Anglo traders met a similar fate.

During the last two decades of Spanish rule, New Mexico was largely untouched by the frequent changes of government in Mexico which took place during the Napoleonic era and the revolution of 1810–1815, although Pedro Bautista Pino was sent as a delegate to the 1812 constitutional *cortes* in Spain. Far removed from events within the capital, the governors attempted to cope with local problems, often unaware that one change in government had taken place before another had occurred since the orders and decrees sent from Mexico were often obsolete before they had arrived in Santa Fe. Plagued by isolation, weakened by campaigns and restricted by trade barriers, New Mexico was in a deplorable condition when Mexico declared her independence from Spain in 1821.

El Comand.te Gral. de las provincias internas de Occidente, à los havitantes de ella.

Amados compatriotas. Ha llegado el dia venturoso destinado por la providencia para que juren ante los Altares la independencia de nuestra Patria. El héroe inmortal D.n Agustin de Yturbide y el voto general de los pueblos esplicado del modo mas energico por toda la estension de la Nueva España, levanta y consolida à un mismo tiempo el grandioso edificio de nuestra libertad. No es posible ciscular los bienes que brotarán y principalmente nuestros sucesores han à conseguir con esta obra que bendecirá el Omnipotente como fundada en los imprescriptibles derechos que concedió à todos los hombres. La Religion santa que profesamos se afirma del modo mas firme: la justicia es inseparable de unas instituciones que la tienen por fundamento: y las ciencias, la prosperidad del comercio y el progreso de la agricultura y de las Artes, son necesariamente los frutos de un Gobierno liberal que se apoya sobre la sana moral y sobre la solida base de la justicia; pero amados compatriotas es necesario que tengais presente que la firme adhesion à las autoridades, la union inseparable de buenos animos, y la mas resuelta determinacion de arrancar de nuestros corazones hasta las mas debiles raices del odio y de la venganza, son medios indispensables para llegar al alto fin à que aspira la independencia. Sea pues nuestra divisa la Religion, y la mas cordial fraternidad, satisfechos de que la felicidad y progreso duradero de las Naciones es solo obra de las virtudes. Chihuahua 27. de Agosto de 1821.

Official Bando of Alejo García Conde, Comandante General,
to the Governor of New Mexico Announcing Mexican Independence
from Spain
State Records Center and Archives

The Mexican Period, 1821–1846

With the signing of the Treaty of Córdova on August 24, 1821, Mexico secured its independence from Spain and New Mexico now became a part of the Mexican nation. The history of the brief twenty-five year period from independence in 1821 to August 18, 1846, when Brigadier-General Stephen Watts Kearny raised the U.S. flag over the venerable Palace of the Governors in Santa Fe, was a troubled one for the northern frontier of New Mexico, due in part to the turmoil within Mexico itself.

In 1822 General Agustín de Iturbide, one of the leaders of the revolution against Spain, had himself crowned as Emperor of Mexico but was removed by revolution a year later. The republicans then assumed power, a congress was assembled, and on October 4, 1824 a federal constitution, modeled closely on that of the United States, was adopted and Guadalupe Victoria was elected president—the first and only president to occupy that office for the full tenure during the period in which New Mexico was attached to Mexico. Behind the scenes was a lesser army official named Antonio López de Santa Anna who cast a long shadow over Mexican political life for the next thirty years, whether in power or temporarily deposed and plotting to return. Civil wars, threats of foreign invasion and constant changes of administration within Mexico resulted in neglect of its dependencies. Directives were regularly sent to the Governor of New Mexico, but often no sooner had instructions arrived from one government until it would have fallen and the next post would bring a new set of orders from the government then in power. Actually, administration in Santa Fe had greater continuity than that in Mexico City since New Mexico officials often had a longer tenure in office.

With independence few changes were made in the legal status and administration of New Mexico. Spanish laws were continued in force where they did not conflict with the new constitution. Even the Spanish governor, Facundo Melgares, continued to hold his job. Until January 31, 1824, New Mexico remained one of the *provincias internas* attached to the *comandancia* of Chihuahua. On that date, the region was joined briefly with Chihuahua and Durango to form the Internal State of the North. With the adoption of the 1824 constitution, Chihuahua and Durango became states and New Mexico was made a territory until 1837. The governor carried the title of *gefe político* and administered civil affairs, while a *comandante principal,* subordinate to the *comandante general* of Chihuahua, was in charge of the military. Governors Antonio Narbona, 1825–1827, and Albino Pérez, 1835–1837, however, combined both civil and military functions. The chief executives were appointed by the national government and with few exceptions, were native New Mexicans, which was a marked departure from Spanish policy. As a result, a powerful group of local families came to dominate New Mexico political affairs.

From 1824 to 1837 the legislative body, known as the *diputación territorial,* functioned more as an advisory council to the executive than as a law-making agency. Throughout the period New Mexicans selected a delegate to the national congress by a system of indirect election. The alcaldes continued to be the chief local officials and presided over the lower courts, and the villages and larger settlements continued to be administered by the elected ayuntamientos.

Perhaps the most far-reaching development during Mexican sovereignty was the abandonment of the Spanish policy of excluding foreign traders which resulted in the opening of the Santa Fe Trail route linking New Mexico with the United States. In the early fall of 1821, William Becknell set out from Franklin, Missouri taking a small load of goods to trade with the Indians of the Rocky Mountains and made his way across Raton Pass where he was met by Mexican troops. Instead of being taken prisoner for entering the territory illegally, he was escorted into Santa Fe to dispose of his goods. By January of 1822 he was back in Franklin, having traded his wares for Mexican silver pesos and fired the enthusiasm of other Missouri River town merchants in the prospects of a new era of trade and commerce with the Spanish Southwest. Becknell returned to Santa Fe in the spring of 1822 by

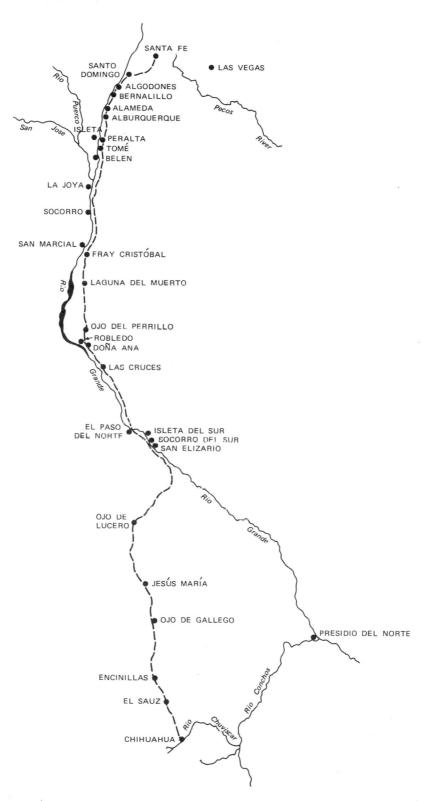

SANTA FE

SANTO
DOMINGO

LAS VEGAS

ALGODONES
BERNALILLO
ALAMEDA
ALBURQUERQUE

Rio

Puerco

Pecos

River

San

Jose

ISLETA

PERALTA
TOMÉ
BELEN

LA JOYA

SOCORRO

SAN MARCIAL

FRAY CRISTÓBAL

Rio

LAGUNA DEL MUERTO

OJO DEL PERRILLO
ROBLEDO
DOÑA ANA

Grande

LAS CRUCES

EL PASO
DEL NORTE

ISLETA DEL SUR
SOCORRO DEL SUR
SAN ELIZARIO

Rio

OJO DE
LUCERO

Grande

JESÚS MARÍA

OJO DE GALLEGO

PRESIDIO DEL NORTE

Rio Conchos

ENCINILLAS

EL SAUZ

Rio

Chuviscar

CHIHUAHUA

The Santa Fe-Chihuahua Trail
State Records Center and Archives Staff

way of the Cimarron Cut-Off route and was soon followed by dozens of Anglo traders and trade caravans in regular succession.

Leading westward from the towns of Franklin, Westport and Leavenworth on the Missouri, the Santa Fe Trail passed through present Kansas to the great bend of the Arkansas River, then along the north bank of that river as far as present Cimarron, Kansas. At this point the route separated, with the northern section, known as the Mountain Branch, continuing along the Arkansas to present La Junta, Colorado where it crossed the river and ran southward over Raton Pass to La Junta (now Watrous) at the junction of the Sapelló and Mora rivers. The Cimarron Cut-Off forded the Arkansas at Cimarron, Kansas and took a direct route to the La Junta crossing where it was joined by the Mountain Branch. Since the Cut-Off was shorter and over relatively level ground, it soon became the major route. Passing through present Las Vegas, the Trail crossed the Pecos River at San Miguel del Vado, which became one of the major towns in New Mexico, and led over Glorieta Pass and through Apache Canyon into the plaza at Santa Fe where goods were unloaded for inspection by officials of the *Aduana* (custom-house). The ruts of the Santa Fe Trail were so deeply engraven into the earth that they would be visible nearly 100 years after the last yoke of oxen or span of mules had plodded into the capital.

By 1824 the sharp increase in trade had broken the monopoly of the Chihuahua merchants since prices of goods from the United States were generally lower and some New Mexico merchants even purchased more from the Anglo traders than they needed and sold the surplus in Chihuahua while the New Mexico treasury, which depended largely on the collection of customs duties, was in a prosperous condition. Soon, the Santa Fe Trail was extended to Chihuahua as the Anglo traders could realize more profits by taking their caravans down the Camino Real into northern Mexico where goods and specie were more abundant. By 1834 economic benefits for New Mexico had declined as Santa Fe had become only the major stopping place for many traders from the United States who sold no goods in New Mexico but took their caravans directly to the Mexican interior. In the meantime, however, New Mexico merchants were profiting from goods which they transported east along the Santa Fe Trail to the Missouri River towns.

Santa Fe became the hub for trade in all directions after 1829 when the route known as the Spanish Trail was finally blazed to

California. On November 6 of that year, Antonio Armijo led a party of thirty traders with a mule train of woolens north from Santa Fe through Abiquiu and following portions of the 1776 Escalante-Domínguez trail, reached San Gabriel Mission near Los Angeles on January 31, 1830, where they traded their goods for horses and mules and returned to Santa Fe. Within the year they were followed by several other groups. In 1831 the first of many herds of sheep was driven from New Mexico to California. In spite of the fact that this long, perilous, winding route could be traveled only by pack caravans, the amount of goods and animals exchanged between New Mexico and California during the next twenty years was extremely important to the people of both frontier outposts of the Mexican Republlic.

Anglo and French-Canadian fur trappers also came in larger numbers because of the quality of beaver in New Mexico streams. Some of these "Mountain Men," as well as many of the traders, blended into the communities, especially at Taos and Santa Fe, became naturalized citizens, married into Mexican families and even held local office, thus adding another ethnic strain to New Mexico culture. In spite of this, however, many of them retained their loyalty to the United States and it was due in part to their influence that occupation in 1846 was relatively easy.

By the 1821 Treaty of Córdova, Indians were granted full citizenship. The designation of genízaro was officially dropped and this group largely amalgamated into the general population. Otherwise, little change in Indian administration was made. Conflicts continued with the Navajos, Apaches and Utes, with depredations on both sides. The Pueblos maintained their traditional way of life and practiced their separate civil and religious customs. The Spanish policy of protecting their lands was continued and they furnished much of the agricultural produce for the larger towns. They also raised their quota of militia troops for military campaigns. Pecos Pueblo continued to decline and in 1838 was abandoned and the last few inhabitants joined their relatives at Jémez.

The decline of the Franciscan Order apparent in the last decades of Spanish rule continued and as the friars died or were recalled, they were replaced by secular priests responsible to the Bishop of Durango. In spite of the fact that Bishop José Antonio Laureano de Zubiría made official visitations in 1833 and 1845 and appointed Father Juan Felipe Ortiz of Santa Fe as his vicar

The Santa Fe Trail
National Park Service

Aerial View of the Mountain Branch of the
Santa Fe Trail near Fort Union
Laura Gilpin

Severino Martinez House, Taos
Richard Federici

for New Mexico, many parishes and missions were vacant throughout the period due to a shortage of secular priests. Compulsory collection of tithes was abolished by the national congress in 1833. As a result, many church structures deteriorated through neglect. Local santeros, however, continued to carve the traditional wooden images of the saints for adornment of chapel altars. The few parish priests were mostly New Mexicans trained in Durango. Some of them, including Father Antonio José Martínez of Taos and José Manuel Gallegos of Albuquerque, took an active part in political affairs and were frequently elected to the various legislative bodies.

A serious attempt was made to establish public schools particularly in the larger towns, but these programs were hampered by the chronic lack of funds. The private school operated by Father Martínez of Taos, however, was responsible for the education of many leaders of both the Mexican and early U.S. territorial periods.

The first printing press was brought into New Mexico along the Santa Fe trail by Josiah Gregg in 1834 and was bought by Ramón Abreú. Some government printing and a few issues of a small newspaper entitled *El Crepúsculo* (The Dawn) were printed on it before it was acquired by Father Martínez who used it to print religious tracts and educational materials for his classrooms. The press was later purchased or leased from Martínez by the authorities in Santa Fe to publish two short-lived government newspapers, *La Verdad* (The Truth) and *El Payo de Nuevo Méjico* (The Countryman of New Mexico), in 1844–1845.

The most serious problem of New Mexico during the Mexican period was the lack of adequate finances to maintain the bare essentials of government. The chief source of revenue was the *derecho de consumo* or excise tax levied on goods imported from the United States. By a special concession from the central government, domestic produce of New Mexico, except for gold and silver bullion, was free of export duty. Until 1828 export of gold or silver in dust or bars was not legal, and although permission was then granted, probably because of the discovery of gold near Santa Fe, it was suspended for silver in 1835. But the traders considered bullion a major part of their return cargo and soon found ways to smuggle it out of the country.

The derecho de consumo was the chief source of funds for all New Mexico governmental activities since the national government was unwilling or unable to furnish financial support from the national treasury. Many early writers, relying on the accounts of the traders, concluded that with the growing commerce over the Santa Fe-Chihuahua Trail in the 1830's and 1840's, increasing amounts of customs duties were collected with much of the funds finding their way into the pockets of local officials, especially those of Governor Manuel Armijo. Undoubtedly, there was some bribery and embezzlement. However, import duties were insufficient to pay for governmental functions, if fully collected, especially as the traders were most ingenious in smuggling their goods into the country and defrauding the customs officials by repacking their cargoes in tremendous loads on fewer wagons at the outskirts of Santa Fe since they were taxed by the load. Thus, the prosperity of the traders was no index to the prosperity of the money-shy New Mexico government.

The only other means of revenue was a voluntary or, in times of extreme military necessity, a forced loan from wealthy citizens. Throughout the period, campaigns were frequent against the Navajos, Apaches and occasionally the Utes. Often, the New Mexico treasury was so depleted that the soldiers had to be paid in corn or wheat.

The economy in the Santa Fe area enjoyed a brief spurt of prosperity with the discovery of gold in the Ortiz Mountains south of the city in 1828 and with a second strike further south in the Tuerto region during the early 1830's. However, these "booms" were short-lived, due largely to primitive methods of extraction.

A complete reorganization of administration occurred in 1836 when the conservative faction gained control of Mexico and imposed a centralist constitution dividing the nation into departments, rather than states and territories. The office of alcalde mayor was abolished in the Department of New Mexico and the former alcaldias were concentrated into two major subdivisions known as *prefecturas,* each headed by a prefect responsible directly to the governor. In 1844 a third prefectura was added to administer the northern area. The territorial diputación was replaced by the *junta departamental* which became the *asamblea departamental,* or departmental assembly, in 1844.

The Departmental Plan was highly unpopular, particularly because Governor Pérez was not a native New Mexican. On August 3, 1837 a full-fledged revolution broke out in the north, centered in the Chimayó-Santa Cruz de la Cañada region and the insurrectionists issued an ultimatum that they would neither

41

permit the establishment of the Departmental Plan nor pay the taxes.

Pérez, unable to suppress the revolution, fled south with his cabinet, but was captured and killed at Agua Fría near Santa Fe. Prefect Santiago Abreú and other members of the cabinet were slain at the Pueblo of Santo Domingo. The rebels installed José González of Ranchos de Taos, a genizaro by ancestry, as governor. Leading citizens of the prefectura of Albuquerque which was largely untouched by the revolt, met and issued the "Plan of Tomé," calling for the overthrow of the insurrectionists and appointed former Governor Manuel Armijo as "Chief of the Liberating Army." Armijo and his forces arrived in Santa Fe on September 12 and reinforced by regular dragoons from Vera Cruz defeated the revolutionists and executed the leaders, including González. Shortly thereafter, Armijo was again appointed governor and in 1839 was also made comandante general responsible directly to the Minister of War in Mexico City rather than to the Comandante of Chihuahua. The central authorities, however, continued to ignore New Mexico. Indian troubles increased, demanding more military expenditures, and a new danger of invasion theatened in 1841 when Mirabeau Lamar, President of the new Republic of Texas, dispatched an expedition under Colonel Hugh McLeod to take possession of the capital of New Mexico and capture the trade caravans of the Santa Fe Trail. Near Anton Chico Armijo's forces captured the remnant of the expedition which had managed to reach New Mexico, and those who were not executed were sent in chains to Mexico City.

For a time Armijo was popular with President Santa Anna who had returned to power in 1841, but economic support was not forthcoming and Indian troubles and threats of invasion increased. On May 1, 1843 Armijo led his forces to the Arkansas River to protect the incoming Santa Fe Trail caravans from the depredations of Texas-based expeditions, but the advance guard was defeated by a group of the raiders and he returned to Santa Fe with the main force. However, a U.S. military detail stationed north of the Arkansas escorted the caravan as far as the New Mexico border.

Later in the year, charges against Armijo of mismanagement, incompetence and dishonesty resulted in an official investigation by General Mariano Monterde with the result that Armijo was replaced by Mariano Martínez, Comandante of Chihuahua.

San Isidro
Museum of New Mexico

Martínez was able, but like Albino Pérez was not a native New Mexican and hence was highly unpopular. He attempted to tighten administration and reform the judicial system. He also stopped the illegal practice of Armijo in alienating the public domain by making large land grants to combines of Anglo-American and native speculators. To feed the army Martínez was forced to borrow money from citizens with repayment guaranteed from the revenue of the Santa Fe Trail caravans. However, the national government closed New Mexico's ports of entry to all trade from September 1844 to March 1845 and the governor had to resort to forced loans. Although trade was resumed in the spring, the financial crisis intensified. Martínez resigned and Manuel Armijo was again appointed governor November 16, 1845.

Rumors of possible U.S. invasion in early 1846 further demoralized the government. Following the declaration by President James K. Polk that a state of war existed between the United States and Mexico, Brigadier-General Stephen Watts Kearny, in late June, led the Army of the West out of Fort Leavenworth, Missouri, for the conquest of New Mexico and California and by July 30 was at Bent's Fort on the Arkansas River in present Colorado. Here he issued a proclamation stating that he was occupying New Mexico and advised that resistance was useless. He then sent former Mexican trader James Magoffin to Santa Fe to treat with Armijo, escorted by Captain Philip St. George Cooke, who held a secret session with the governor on August 12. To meet the invaders Armijo marched his demoralized, unpaid army of regulars, militia and the Vera Cruz squadron of dragoons east of the city and began to fortify Apache Canyon, but changed his mind and without offering resistance to the invaders, fled southward, first to Albuquerque, then to Chihuahua taking the dragoons with him. Late in the afternoon of August 18, a tired Army of the West marched into Santa Fe. The colors of the Mexican Republic were hauled down and the U.S. flag run up over the Palace of the Governors. Acting governor Juan Bautista Vigil y Alaríd officially surrendered New Mexico to the United States.

AVISO.

HALLANDOME debidamente antorizado por el Presidente de los Estados Unidos de America, por la presente hago los Siguientes nombramientos para la gobernacion de Nuevo Mejico, Territorio de los Estados Unidos.

Los Empleados asi nombrados seran obedecidos y respetados segun corresponde.

CARLOS BENT Será GOBERNADOR,
Donaciano Vigil " Secretario del Territorio,
Ricardo Dallum " Esherif mayor (alguacil
Francisco P. Blair" Promotor fiscal, [mayor)
Carlos Blumner" " Tesorero
Eugenio Leitensdorfer " Yntendente de cu entas públicas,
Joab Houghton, Antonio José Otero y Carlos Beaubien seran Jués de la Suprema Cortede Justicia y cada uno en su District seran jues de circuito.

Dado en Santa Fé capital del terri de Nuevo Mejico este dia á 22 de de Setiembre 1846, y el 71 ° de la Indepencia de los Estados Unidos·
S. W KEARNY,
General de Brigada
del Egercito de los E. Unidos.

NOTICE.

BEING duly authorized by the President of the United States of America, I hereby make the following appointments for the Government of New Mexico, a territory of the United States.

The officers thus appointed will be obeyed and respected accordingly·

CHARLES BENT to be Governor.
Donaciano Vigil " Sec. of Territory.
Richard Dallam " Marshall.
Francis P Blair " U. S. D . A .'y
Charles Blummer " Treasurer.
Eugene Leitensdorfer " Aud. of Pub. Acc.
Joal Houghton, Antonio José Otero, Charles Beaubien to be Judges of "the Superior Court."

Given at Santa Fe, the Capitol of the Territory of New Mexico, this 22d day of September 1846 and in the 71st year of the Independence of the United States.

S. W. KEARNY,
Brig. General
U. S. Army.

Kearny Proclamation, September 22, 1846
State Records Center and Archives

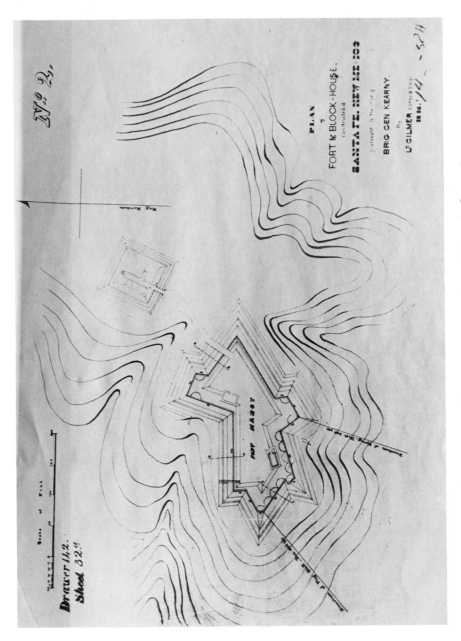

1846 Plan for the Construction of Fort Marcy in Santa Fe
State Records Center and Archives

New Mexico Since 1846

Occupation of New Mexico was peaceful. On August 19, 1846, in the plaza of Santa Fe, Kearny, as he had done at each settlement along the route, read a proclamation informing the inhabitants that New Mexico was now a Territory of the United States of which they were citizens. He promised that they would be protected in their property and civil rights so long as they did not resist the change in sovereignty. He immediately ordered a fort to be built in case of resistance and on August 23 the construction of Fort Marcy, located 600 yards from the plaza on the eminence commanding the city, was begun. Although this massive, adobe star-shaped fort with its log blockhouse was the first U.S. military post constructed in the Southwest, it was never garrisoned, needed or used. The barracks, corrals and other facilities were located adjacent to the Palace of the Governors as they had been under Spain and Mexico, and the name of Fort Marcy came to be applied to the military post which took shape north of the plaza.

Delegations from many of the Pueblos soon came to Santa Fe to pledge their allegiance to the new government and were promised protection from the Navajos. On September 22 Kearny appointed civil officials for New Mexico headed by Charles Bent of Taos as governor and promulgated the "Organic Law of the Territory," a codification of Spanish-Mexican and U.S. Law popularly known as the Kearny Code. Both of these documents were printed on the old Martínez press. President Polk in December, however, repudiated the right of a general to confer territorial status on an occupied area or make the residents of New Mexico citizens of the United States since these were powers reserved to the federal congress.

Immediately after providing for the administration of New

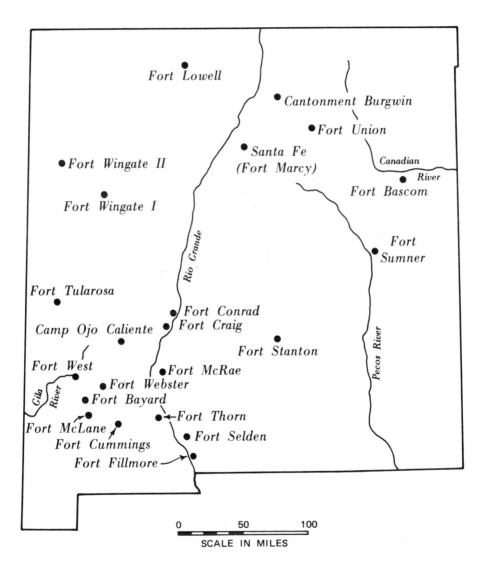

Fort Lowell

Cantonment Burgwin

Fort Union

Santa Fe
(Fort Marcy)

Canadian
River

Fort Bascom

Fort Wingate II

Fort Wingate I

Rio Grande

Fort
Sumner

Fort Tularosa

Fort Conrad
Fort Craig

Camp Ojo Caliente

Fort Stanton

Pecos River

Fort West

Fort McRae

Gila River

Fort Webster

Fort Bayard

Fort Thorn

Fort McLane

Fort Selden

Fort Cummings

Fort Fillmore

0   50   100

SCALE IN MILES

U.S. Forts in New Mexico

Mexico, Kearny led the main army south along the Rio Grande through the Jornada del Muerto to present Rincon, then struck westward through New Mexico and southern Arizona for the conquest of California leaving Colonel Sterling Price in charge at Santa Fe. Colonel A. W. Doniphan led an expedition northwest and signed a treaty with the Navajos at Bear Springs, present Fort Wingate, on November 22, then marched south along the Camino Real to reinforce U.S. forces fighting in Chihuahua. On Christmas Day, 1846 he defeated Mexican troops at Brazitos, near Las Cruces, the only engagement of the Mexican War which was fought on New Mexico soil.

While occupation had been bloodless and the great majority of New Mexicans, both Hispano and Pueblo Indian, had accepted the change in sovereignty willingly, some of the native leaders remained loyal to their former mother country. Soon after the main body of U.S. troops had left Santa Fe, groups of conspirators began to plan an uprising to recapture New Mexico for the Mexican Republic. In December a plot to retake Santa Fe was discovered by the authorities. On January 19, 1847 at the village of Don Fernando de Taos, however, a band of nationalists joined by Taos Pueblo Indians who were fearful that the new government would interfere with their land rights attacked the Anglo-Americans and their Mexican families, killing most of the local officials and Governor Charles Bent who was visiting his family. They then stormed north to Arroyo Hondo and wiped out the establishment of trader and distiller Simeon Turley. Another uprising took place at Mora. Colonel Sterling Price with the U.S. troops and a Mountain Man militia company enlisted in Santa Fe by Cerán St. Vrain marched north subduing armed bands of insurrectionists at Santa Cruz and Embudo. At Taos they found the rebels entrenched within the thick adobe walls of the mission of San Gerónimo. In the bombardment which followed, the church was virtually demolished. The revolt was quickly suppressed and some of the participants, after a short trial, were executed for murder or treason, in spite of the fact that federal authorities had not yet made New Mexicans citizens of the United States.

After the death of Bent, native-born Donanciano Vigil, who had been appointed Secretary of the Territory by Kearny, became acting civil governor, subordinate to Military Governor Price until the signing of the Treaty of Guadalupe Hidalgo in 1848 officially transferring New Mexico, together with other Southwestern areas, to the United States. Under its terms New Mexicans could choose to become citizens of the United States or retain their Mexican citizenship, but in either case their property and civil rights were to be protected. Official incorporation into the union, however, was left to the discretion of Congress and military governors continued to administer the area. In the summer of 1850, a constitutional convention adopted a plan for statehood, but Congress paid no attention and on September 9 created the Territory of New Mexico. Texas was paid $10,000,000 to relinquish its claim to the region east of the Rio Grande. James S. Calhoun, who had been serving as Indian Superintendent, was appointed the first territorial governor.

In 1853 the present boundaries of the continental United States were completed when a large tract of land in southwestern New Mexico and Arizona, known as the Gadsden Purchase, was bought from Mexico for another $10,000,000.

The decade preceding the Civil War was characterized by increased westward expansion into the regions recently acquired from Mexico. Some immigrants remained in New Mexico and travel routes were greatly expanded especially after the discovery of the California gold fields. The major stagecoach line was that of The Butterfield Overland Mail Company which operated from St. Louis to San Francisco and crossed the southern part of New Mexico. Additional troops were stationed in the territory to protect the new settlers, and forts were built to guard the lines of communications since confrontations with the Navajos and Apaches continued. Among these were Fort Union, north of Las Vegas, to protect the Santa Fe Trail; Fort Fillmore near Mesilla and Fort Craig at the northern end of the Jornada del Muerto to protect the Rio Grande route; Fort Stanton on the Rio Bonito; and Fort Fauntleroy at the Ojo del Oso at the north end of the Zuni Mountains on the edge of Navajo country.

With the secession of the southern states from the Union in the spring of 1861, most of the ranking army officials in New Mexico resigned their commissions and left the territory to offer their services to the Confederacy. In an attempt to sever the Southwest from the Union and secure the gold fields of California and Colorado, Confederate forces from Texas invaded New Mexico. Mesilla was occupied in July 1861, and in January 1862 Brigadier-General H. H. Sibley led his forces out of Fort Bliss (present El Paso) and up the Rio Grande. On February 21–22 he defeated the few Army regulars and the territorial volunteers of Colonel E. R. S. Canby at the Battle of Valverde, and by-passing Fort Craig, marched through Albuquerque and occupied Santa Fe on March 23. Unionist Governor Henry Connelly, however, had already moved his headquarters to Las Vegas and Sibley now advanced towards Fort Union, the guardian of the Santa Fe Trail.

U.S. Army regulars, reenforced by New Mexico militia units and the Colorado Volunteers, however, were marching westward from Fort Union to the relief of Colonel Canby. The forces met near Glorieta Pass where the southerners were defeated on March 26—28 in a battle often called "The Gettysburg of the West." They retreated south, pursued by the Union forces through Albuquerque where they were also met by Colonel Canby and the troops from Fort Craig. After a second defeat at Peralta, April 14—15, the Confederates continued their retreat down the Rio Grande.

Meanwhile, General James H. Carleton commanding a body of California Volunteers was marching across the deserts of southern California and Arizona to assist in actions against the Confederates. By late August 1862 he had taken possession of Mesilla and Las Cruces and reoccupied Fort Fillmore. New Mexico remained Union territory. On September 18 Carleton replaced Canby as Commander of the Department.

With the sectional conflict ended, territorial and federal authorities turned their attention to military action against the Apaches and Navajos who, feeling increasing pressures of continued intrusion into their lands, stepped up their raids on livestock herds and against settlers and prospectors. One by one the various groups of these Indians were defeated and placed on reservations. General Carleton ordered concerted action against them soon after his arrival in Santa Fe. In 1862 Fort Stanton was reoccupied and Fort Sumner built on the Pecos River at the region known as the Bosque Redondo to serve against the Mescalero Apaches, and Fort Wingate established on the Ojo del Gallo near present San Rafael for action against the Navajos. The following year, 1863, Fort Cummings was located near Cooke's Spring to protect the Mesilla-Tucson route and Fort McRae at the northern end of the Jornada del Muerto to safeguard the Rio Grande route, followed by Fort Selden in 1865 at the southern end of the Jornada.

Militia Colonel Christopher (Kit) Carson, placed in charge of the military forces by Carleton, first concentrated his action against the Mescalero Apaches who were largely subdued by the

Aerial View of Fort Selden
Jerry Goffee

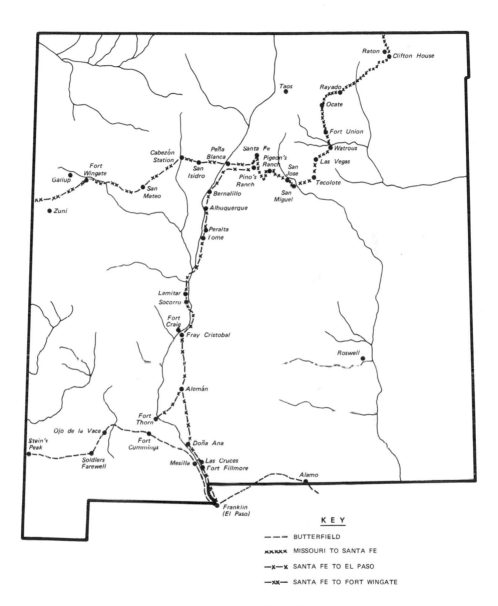

Raton
Clifton House
Taos
Rayado
Ocate
Fort Union
Cabezón
Station
Peña
Blanca
Santa Fe
Pigeon's
Ranch
Watrous
Las Vegas
Fort
Wingate
San
Isidro
Pino's
Ranch
San
Jose
Gallup
San
Mateo
Bernalillo
San
Miguel
Tecolote
Zuni
Albuquerque
Peralta
Tome
Lemitar
Socorro
Fort
Craig
Fray Cristobal
Roswell
Alemán
Fort
Thorn
Ojo de la Vaca
Stein's
Peak
Fort
Cummings
Doña Ana
Soldiers
Farewell
Mesilla
Las Cruces
Fort Fillmore
Alamo
Franklin
(El Paso)

K E Y

– – – BUTTERFIELD
xxxxx MISSOURI TO SANTA FE
—x—x SANTA FE TO EL PASO
—xx— SANTA FE TO FORT WINGATE

*Main Stagecoach Routes in New Mexico
State Records Center and Archives Staff*

53

Shakespeare Ghost Town

summer of 1863 and placed on the Bosque Redondo reservation. Carson, assisted by Lt. Col. J. Francisco Chaves commanding at Fort Wingate, then turned his attention to the Navajos. A two-year campaign by rounding up individual bands and sending them to the Bosque Redondo in the "Long Walk," combined with the systematic destruction of Indian crops and confiscation of livestock, effectively broke Navajo resistance.

The Bosque Redondo reservation was no lasting solution to the problem as the area would not support the Indian population. The crops failed, the livestock died, government supplies were insufficient and Navajos and Apaches were often at odds with each other. In November 1865, the Mescaleros deserted the reservation en masse and scattered in small bands but gradually returned to the Fort Stanton area. A permanent reservation was created for them in the White and Sacramento Mountains in 1873. Difficulties with the western Apache tribes who particularly menaced the mining regions continued, however, and in 1866 Fort Bayard was established east of Silver City to protect the Pinos Altos mining district. The capture of Chiricahua chieftain Geronimo in 1886 finally ended the long period of Indian warfare in New Mexico.

Meanwhile, conditions for the Navajos at Bosque Redondo had also become intolerable and in 1868 they were permitted to return to their Four Corners homeland where a permanent reservation was established for them. Fort Wingate at San Rafael was abandoned and the garrison transferred to old Fort Fauntleroy on the Ojo del Oso which was reactivated under the name of Fort Wingate.

Following the Civil War, livestock became the dominant industry in the western valleys and also in the Llano Estacado east of the Pecos River where the forts and the Bosque Redondo reservation provided a ready market for beef. In 1866 Charles Goodnight and Oliver Loving trailed the first of many herds of Texas cattle to the Horsehead Crossing of the Pecos south of present Carlsbad and up the valley to the Fort Sumner area. Other west Texas cattlemen moved into the region and by the 1870's the cattle drives had become virtual stampedes, particularly after the Comanches had been subdued and the hide hunters had exterminated the buffalo.

Sheep-raising, which had been the major economy of the New Mexican since the Spanish period, also thrived as new markets were opened. Soon, western flocks were being driven on to range in

Arizona and Hispano stockmen from the Las Vegas region moved into the Llano Estacado and established the traditional settlement placitas. By the 1870's the midwestern and Rocky Mountain states were stocked with New Mexico sheep.

The livestock development was not always peaceful. The sheepmen often fought with cattlemen and the cattle barons fought one another. With the opening up of large areas of the public domain to farmers under the Homestead Act, cattlemen attempted to keep the "nesters" off the open range. The violent Lincoln County range war of the 1870's, complicated by political rivalries and overtones, was ended only by the use of federal troops during the administration of Governor Lew. Wallace.

By the early 1880's both eastern U.S. and foreign capital were attracted into the lucrative livestock business, especially in eastern New Mexico, but the boom period ended late in the decade due to a sharp decline in cattle prices combined with extended drought and harsh winters. With the influx of farmers and the end of the open range, both ranchers and settlers were enclosing their holdings with barbed wire and utilizing the windmill for water supply. The coming of the railroads had also lessened the need for long drives to market. As the brief period of mining prosperity declined with the depletion of high-grade ores in the southwestern mountainous regions, the more stable livestock industry often took its place. By 1885 the once booming Kelly mining district west of Socorro was being overshadowed by nearby Magdalena, rail head terminus of the great annual cattle and sheep drives through the more than 100-mile long San Agustin Plains.

Most of the small farmers who came into the plains regions in increasing numbers during the last quarter of the century to homestead soon found the 160-acre allotments totally inadequate to make a living and lost or sold their claims. Larger agricultural enterprises, however, prospered where irrigation was possible. After 1877 the rich bottom land of the San Juan Valley was settled by farmers as well as stockmen. By 1890 wells were being drilled to tap the springs of the Artesian Basin of the Pecos River for irrigation, and in 1891 Charles B. Eddy, Charles Green and James J. Hagerman organized the Pecos Irrigation Project to develop the valley by utilizing the artesian wells and waters impounded from the Pecos River in the Avalon and MacMillan dams. The operation proved to be too ambitious for private capital, and in

1906 the Federal Reclamation Service purchased the holdings for the Carlsbad Reclamation Project.

In 1903 the Federal Reclamation Service also began a comprehensive program of dam construction on the Rio Grande for the promotion of irrigation, culminating in the completion of Elephant Butte Dam in 1916, followed soon by other similar smaller structures.

While exploitation of the public domain was proceeding at a fast pace in the regions opened to settlement for the first time after the Civil War, the problem of title to large areas of land in northern New Mexico which had been settled by Spanish colonists and held by their descendants long before U.S. occupation was much more difficult to solve. The 1848 Treaty of Guadalupe Hidalgo with Mexico had stipulated that property rights which were legally held under Mexican law would be respected by the United States. The Spanish land tenure system as developed in New Mexico and continued by Mexico after the 1821 revolution was, however, far different from the English-American concept of private land ownership which had been developed in the eastern United States and was brought to New Mexico with occupation. Under Spain and Mexico the governors of New Mexico had been authorized to provide for the expanding population by making grants of unappropriated domain for agricultural and grazing purposes to landless private individuals and groups of settlers who would establish communities, usually on the frontiers, to serve as buffers against hostile Indian attack. Familiar landmarks such as mesas, arroyos and trees rather than explicit surveys were used to designate the boundaries of the grants. Title in fee simple was given to private grantees who fulfilled the legal terms of their grants, but in the community grants individual title was given only for the farming lands allotted to each settler and the remainder of the land used for grazing was held in common. In all cases, however, Spanish law required that the grants were not to encroach on the lands of the Indian Pueblos. For the most part, this protection of Indian land was scrupulously observed. Due to the indefinite nature of boundary limits the grants often overlapped one another.

Because of the chaotic conditions during the closing years of the Mexican regime, confusion prevailed over land title at the time of occupation, a situation which worsened as new settlers came into

Laureano Cordova Mill
Karl Kernberger

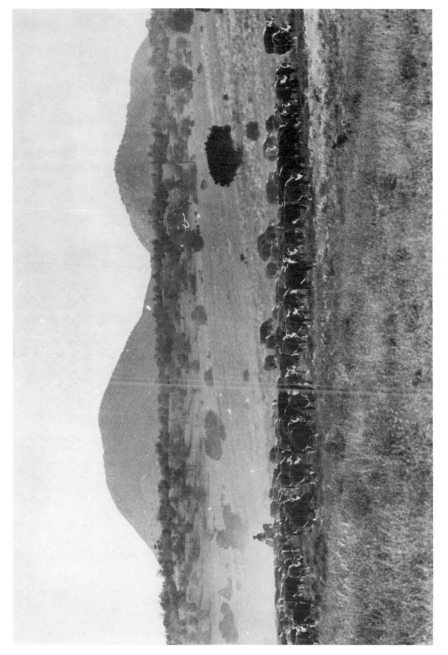

Moving Cattle along the Magdalena Stock Driveway
Bureau of Land Management

Detailed View of Stone Portion of Dorsey Mansion
Robert S. Nugent

Pinckney R. Tully House, Santa Fe
Karl Kernberger

New Mexico. In spite of the provisions of the 1848 treaty no action was taken by the U.S. either to clarify the land title problem or the status of the Pueblo Indians as to whether they were citizens or wards of the government until 1854 when Congress created the Office of Surveyor-General in an attempt to adjudicate Spanish-Mexican titles. Upon approval of the Surveyor-General and confirmation by Congress, the grants were to be surveyed and patents given to the descendants of the grantees or their legitimate successors. In the meantime, however, grant papers had been lost, some had been fraudulently manufactured. Many claimants, often victims of sharp practices, had conveyed their rights to speculators. Surveys revealed the endless conflict of overlapping grants. The courts, unfamiliar with Spanish law and practice, established the precedent that the title to the community grant commons could be divided among the many claimants in partition suits.

Only a few claims were confirmed and patented under the Surveyor-General, and by the 1880's speculation in the grants and public domain had reached the point of a national scandal. In 1891 the Court of Private Land Claims was created to settle the problem by judicial procedure, and by 1903 all land grant claims were adjudicated. The precedent that the commons could also be partitioned and conveyed was continued. As a result much of the land formerly used by the residents of the community land grants for livestock grazing was conveyed to outsiders or was returned to the public domain, to be incorporated into the national forests, leaving a legacy of bitterness among many of the Hispano citizens of the northern counties. Since the Pueblo Indians were not considered as wards of the government until the U.S. Supreme Court "Sandoval Decision" of 1913, their claims were usually not represented before the Court of Private Land Claims and as a result they lost some of their lands which had long been protected by Spanish and Mexican authorities. In some cases, restitution or compensation was later made to them by the decisions of the Pueblo Lands Board created by Congress in 1924 to clarify Indian title and by decisions of the U.S. Indian Claims Commission established in 1948.

Some prospecting had been done before the Civil War, but the real impetus to mining came with the 1866 discovery of rich gold placers in both the Pinos Altos region of the southwestern Black Range and in the north on the western side of Mt. Baldy near Elizabethtown in the upper Moreno Valley of the Maxwell Land

61

Grant. These discoveries were followed in 1869 by the Chloride Flat silver strike at Silver City and the discovery of silver, lead and zinc at Kelly near Socorro. Soon, mining districts dotted the mountain areas of the entire territory, especially in the southwestern portion, in spite of the threat from the Apaches who resented these new intrusions into their traditional hunting lands. New towns sprang up over night as miners and enterprising suppliers of their wants flocked into the mining camps. Often they prospered briefly only to become virtual ghost towns within a few years as the ores were exhausted. One of these was Shakespeare, near the Mexican border, first known as Ralston, where gold was discovered in the nearby Pyramid Mountains also in 1869. After a slump in the 1870's, these mines were revived briefly in 1879. Gold strikes on the slope of Baxter Mountain in Lincoln County resulted in the establishment of White Oaks in 1879. New strikes continued in the Black Range with the discovery of gold at Hillsboro in 1877, silver at Kingston in 1883 and the opening of the fabled Bridal Chamber silver mine at Lake Valley four years later. In 1889 silver was discovered at Mogollon.

Until well into the present century when the supply was exhausted, turquoise continued to be mined in the Cerrillos district south of Santa Fe, probably the oldest continously mined region in the United States, for the Indians were extracting the blue stone before the arrival of the Spaniards. Gold mining had a brief revival in the Ortiz and Tuerto Mountains further to the south, the scene of similar attempts between 1828 and 1834, but difficulties of extraction and litigation over title soon brought a halt to these attempts.

By 1890 the high-grade gold and silver bearing ores were largely exhausted and the mining boom was over, especially after the demonetization of silver in 1893. White Oaks was able to hold out until 1904 when the drop in production, combined with loss of the railroad, caused its mines to close also. The mines of Mogollon continued to operate until 1917.

As the extraction of precious metals sharply declined, copper mining, especially in the old Santa Rita district east of Silver City first developed by Spanish miners from Chihuahua about 1804, continued to be a less exciting but more stable source of mineral productions as did lead and zinc originally found in conjunction with gold and silver ores.

Development of the coal fields around Gallup, Raton and at

Madrid in the Cerrillos district accounted for much of mining activity until after World War II. Potash extraction became the chief industry in the Carlsbad region. The discovery of oil on the Navajo reservation and in the Artesia area in the 1920's soon resulted in the development of one of New Mexico's most important businesses and encouraged the growth of Hobbs, Lovington and other cities of the Permian Basin. The location of rich uranium ores in the Grants area in the early 1950's soon made New Mexico the chief supplier for atomic energy projects.

A virtual commercial revolution characterized New Mexico economic history after U.S. occupation throughout the rest of the century as the small shop-keepers and Santa Fe-Chihuahua Trail traders were replaced by sedentary merchants. Most of these early businessmen were German-Jewish immigrants, representatives of a culture which had been particularly successful in mercantile pursuits in Europe for several generations. The first of these was Jacob Solomon Spiegelberg who came to Santa Fe in the supply train of General Kearny in 1846, went to Mexico with the forces of Colonel Doniphan, then returned to Santa Fe to become sutler at Fort Marcy and was joined by his four brothers in the prospering family enterprise. Soon other Jewish merchants entered the New Mexico field.

Because of its rapidly expanding economy New Mexico also attracted non-Jewish merchants such as German-born Franz Huning who arrived in Albuquerque in 1857 and then expanded his interests into the nearby Rio Grande town of Los Lunas. Many others came in the 1860's. New Mexicans, including Felipe Chavez of Belen, the powerful Otero family in the Rio Grande valley and the Delgados of Santa Fe, were influential in business but most of the merchant capitalists had learned their talents elsewhere and were drawn to New Mexico. Perhaps the most important factor in the economic transformation which resulted, especially after the Civil War, was the ability of the mercantile houses to operate on a wide credit basis with both their retail outlets in the towns and with their suppliers in eastern financial centers. Much foreign capital also came into New Mexico during the 1880's.

Itinerant traders, however, continued to supply many of the needs of smaller and more isolated areas. The Lebanese-born peddler with his pack of small items on his back was a familiar and welcome sight in many small communities into the present century.

By the 1870's even larger credit organizations were needed to finance the livestock, agricultural and mining industries and commercial banks, often with some of the merchants as organizers, were chartered to supplement and later to partially supplant the mercantile firms as credit organizations.

New Mexico's rapidly advancing economy created a need for better and faster transportation resulting in the extension of stage lines during the 1860's and early 1870's and the coming of the railroad. At first, the territory was but a part of great railroad corporate projects for interstate and transcontinental routes which passed through it. The first of these giants was the Atchison, Topeka & Santa Fe. By the summer of 1878 its lines had been extended through western Kansas and eastern Colorado, following the route of the Mountain Branch of the Santa Fe Trail, to Trinidad, Colorado. After a brief encounter with the Denver and Rio Grande Railway Company over Raton Pass, the AT&SF secured the right of way and on April 4, 1879 its first train rolled into Las Vegas. A year later the line was extended to Albuquerque but because of its mountainous location and the expenses of grade construction Santa Fe itself was by-passed by the main line and Albuquerque became the chief railroad terminus quickly surpassing the old capital in economic activity and growth. The Santa Fe Trail had come to an end.

Following the Rio Grande and the route of the Camino Real through the Jornada del Muerto, the AT&SF within another year reached Rincon where it divided with one section continuing on to El Paso. On March 8, 1881 the other branch joined the Southern Pacific, which had been constructed east from California, at Deming, thus forming the second transcontinental route. Meanwhile, its affiliate, the Atlantic and Pacific Railroad, was also building a more direct route to California from Albuquerque northwestward across the Continental Divide then west through Arizona. In 1889, due to importance of nearby coal mines, Gallup became the division terminal of this line.

At the same time, the Denver and Rio Grande Western Railroad, blocked in its attempt to secure passage over Raton Pass, was developing its narrow gauge route into New Mexico from a different direction, one branch of which finally did reach Santa Fe. Pushing westward through southern Colorado its rails were laid to Antonito on the New Mexico border in 1879. From that point one branch, later dubbed the "Chili Line" because of the quantity of peppers raised in the region, led south reaching Española in 1880. By an agreement of that year with the AT&SF to limit construction, however, the line was discontinued at this point, but a group of local promoters organized the Texas, Santa Fe and Northern to complete the last 34 miles between the capital and Española. In 1887, after much delay, Santa Fe at last had a major railroad. Title was finally transferred back to the D&RGW in 1895 and the Chili Line continued to operate until 1941.

At the same time, mining operations in the San Juan Basin of Colorado encouraged the D&RGW to push construction on the other main branch to Durango. Crossing and recrossing the Colorado-New Mexico border over the steepest grades in railroad construction at a cost as high at $140,000 a mile, the railroad reached Chama at the end of 1880, then continued through the coal mining area of Monero arriving at Durango in July of 1881. The two routes of the D&RGW, with their many short branch lines and connecting spurs, made possible the lumbering exploitation of the vast timber resources in northern New Mexico. In 1969 the railroad was given permission to abandon the famous narrow gauge line but the Antonito-Chama portion was jointly purchased by the states of New Mexico and Colorado and is now operated as a tourist attraction.

Within the brief space of two years (1879-1881) nearly one-third of the total railroad mileage in New Mexico had been built. Construction of major lines slackened until after the turn of the century although the Colorado and Southern, linking Colorado and Texas through northeastern New Mexico, was completed in 1888. Within the territory, however, many short lines rapidly spread a network serving livestock, agricultural and mining interests and developing the new coal mining and lumber industries.

The railroad was brought to the Pecos valley by Eddy and Hagerman to link the lands covered by their irrigation project to main lines in Texas. The new town of Eddy (now Carlsbad) was reached in 1891 and Roswell in 1894. A few years later the Pecos system came under control of the AT&SF. The El Paso and Northeastern railroad syndicate of Charles B. Eddy was also responsible for the development of the Tularosa Basin. Beginning from El Paso, the rails reached Eddy's new townsite of Alamogordo in 1898. One branch, built over steep grades to tap the rich timber of the Sacramento Mountains, soon found a second major use in the development of Cloudcroft, entered by a spectacular curved trestle, as a flourishing tourist resort. The major branch was constructed north through Carrizozo and in 1902 joined the just-completed main line of the Chicago, Rock Island and Pacific at Santa Rosa.

Eddy's main purpose had been to develop the White Oaks-Capitan coal resources but when production in this area proved to be less than expected, he turned to the wealthier deposits in Colfax County. Buying out the interest of rancher John B. Dawson who, with his brother had settled on the Vermejo River in 1867, the railroad promoter organized the Dawson Railway to connect the vast coal field to the Rock Island at Tucumcari. However, in 1905 he sold the mines and railroad system to the Phelps-Dodge Corporation which had also secured control of the El Paso and Southwestern Railroad from its Arizona copper mines to El Paso. Until about 1950 when conversion to diesel finally caused the abandonment of Dawson, coal and coke from northern New Mexico were the chief sources of energy for the corporation's great copper empire.

Many other local short lines were built during these years into gold and silver, coal mining and lumber regions but most of these industrial lines have disappeared.

Far-reaching cultural and social changes also took place during the latter half of the 19th century as more and more people of differing economic, social and ethnic backgrounds poured into New Mexico disrupting the relatively uncomplicated Pueblo Indian and Hispanic bicultural society. Since most of the new-comers, even those from foreign countries, spoke English, the term "Anglo" came to be generally applied to all of these groups regardless of their national origins. One of the most significant cultural developments was the disruption of the religious unity of the older groups for although the Pueblos practiced many of their tribal religious customs they, like the Hispanos, were nominally Roman Catholic.

With occupation came not only separation of church and state but also a change in national jurisdiction with the hierarchy of the Roman Catholic Church. In 1851 French-born Jean Baptiste Lamy was sent to New Mexico by United States ecclesiastical authorities as Vicar Apostolic. Two years later New Mexico was separated from the Mexican Diocese of Durango and made a diocese with Lamy as bishop. The new prelate initiated a vigorous

66

program of filling the vacant parishes and missions with priests recruited in European countries, especially France, and imported teaching orders to establish schools. In 1852 he brought the Sisters of Loretto who established a girls' academy in Santa Fe. Members of the Christian Brothers arrived from France in 1859 to found St. Michael's College in the capital. Other church schools soon followed in the major towns.

Attempts to institute changes in local Hispanic church practices and supervise more closely the actions of the few native clergy, however, led to serious disagreements and resulted in the excommunications of several priests, especially Antonio José Martínez of Taos and José Manuel Gallegos of Albuquerque. Lamy and his successors also discouraged the activities of lay organizations known as *Los Hermanos de Luz* (The Brothers of Light), popularly called *Penitentes* because of their continuation of the medieval practice of flagellation. These confraternities, which had developed in the outlying settlements during the Mexican period, maintained their practices, especially Holy Week ceremonies, in the their separate *moradas* (meeting houses) as they were denied the use of regular church buildings.

Bishop Lamy also undertook an ambitious church building program, importing French contractors and artisans for many of the projects. Two of the most significant structures in Santa Fe were the stone Romanesque Cathedral of St. Francis and the Gothic chapel of Our Lady of Light to serve the Sisters of Loretto. New Mexico was elevated to archdiocesan status in 1875.

Protestant denominations also viewed New Mexico as a promising missionary and educational field. Baptist missionary Hiram W. Reed came to Santa Fe in 1849, followed shortly by three fellow ministers who attempted to establish congregations and day schools. In 1854 the Baptists built the first Protestant church building in New Mexico, an adobe chapel in Santa Fe, which was also used by missionaries of other groups until 1866 when the Presbyterians purchased the land and building. Methodist and Presbyterian missionaries were also in the territory in the 1850's, but permanent Protestant establishments came with the rapid expansion of population after the Civil War. The Rt. Rev. Josiah C. Talbot, Bishop of the Northwest, made a missionary visitation of New Mexico in 1863 and held the first services of the Episcopal Church at Fort Union and Santa Fe, but formal organization of congregations was delayed for several years. The Presbyterians,

Cumbres and Toltec Scenic Railroad Station, Chama
Daniel E. Reiley

Trinity Site, Test Excavations in November 1945, around Base of Tower from which Bomb was suspended at Zero Point

National Park Service

from headquarters established at Santa Fe in 1866, were active in founding churches and day schools. Methodist minister Thomas Harwood arrived at Watrous in 1871 and for the next quarter of a century was responsible for much activity of that faith. The Congregational Church was formally organized in 1880. By 1900 all of the major Protestant denominations were firmly established throughout the territory.

A battalion composed of members of The Church of Jesus Christ of Latter Day Saints, commonly known as Mormons, marched through New Mexico in 1846 as a part of the forces of Col. Philip St. George Cooke. During the 1870's Mormon families from Utah migrated into western New Mexico and established several colonies, among them Ramah located in the midst of a small band of Navajos who had settled there after their return from the Fort Sumner reservation.

Because of the lack of a public school system, illiteracy was extremely high in spite of the educational efforts of both Catholic and Protestant church-oriented schools until 1891 when free public education became law. Two years before, reform Governor Edmund G. Ross signed a bill creating the University of New Mexico at Albuquerque, the Agricultural College at Las Cruces and the School of Mines at Socorro. In 1898 Delegate to Congress Harvey B. Fergusson obtained grants of public lands for schools and institutions of higher learning.

New Mexico has also had a long tricultural heritage in the arts which continues into the present. Pueblo Indians, using native cotton, had developed weaving as well as pottery and basket-making before the conquest. With the introduction of sheep by the Spaniards, the Pueblos, and later the Navajos, became proficient in the weaving of blankets for their own use and for trade. After the introduction of machine-made blankets in the late 1880's, the Navajos turned their skills to the making of the distinctive rugs for which they are still famous. About the same time, both Pueblos and Navajos also became skilled silversmiths and since then jewelry production has been a major Indian craft. The revival of excellent pottery making in the 1920's, especially by the Pueblo of San Ildefonso, has caused the products of this age-old art to become world famous.

The varied New Mexico landscape, Indian cultures and Hispanic villages early attracted Anglo artists who traveled through the territory sketching and painting their impressions. In 1898 painters Ernest L. Blumenschein and Bert G. Phillips arrived at Taos and were soon joined by other well known artists who founded the Taos Art Colony, and in 1914 the Taos Society of Artists. By 1920 a permanent artists' colony was established in Santa Fe whose members were known as The Santa Fe Artists Club, and the following year five new Santa Fe artists organized as "Los Cinco Pintores" to exhibit their works. Other artist organizations in the capital came into being in the 1930's. The New Mexico Art League was organized in Albuquerque in 1929. During these years the founding of several institutions for the encouragement of the arts also helped make New Mexico a cultural center of national importance. Among these were the Santa Fe Art Museum built in 1917, a major division of the Museum of New Mexico; the Harwood Gallery in Taos, first established in 1925 but operated by the University of New Mexico as a summer art school after 1930; and the establishment of the Art Department at the University of New Mexico in 1928. Artists have continued to be attracted to these towns in recent years.

Events and developments following U.S. occupation were also reflected in New Mexico architecture. At first, new materials, tools and techniques brought in by the Anglos were employed to modify the existing Spanish-Pueblo structures, but gradually these changes resulted in the evolution of a distinct style known as Territorial. Somewhat influenced by the current Greek Revival movement then popular in the middle west, Territorial characteristics were used in the construction of new buildings and the remodeling of many older structures some of which dated back into the 1700's. One of the best examples of early Territorial construction is the Pinckney R. Tully house in Santa Fe, built in 1851 by a Santa Fe Trail trader, while the best preserved 19th century hacienda type remodeled residence is Los Luceros, north of Española. Thick adobe walls continued to be basic, but sawed lumber was extensively used for floors and ceiling beams. Glass windows were installed in new buildings and cut through walls for remodeling of older structures. Window and door trim of milled lumber featured the characteristic triangular lintel. Mill-sawed posts with a variety of wooden moldings replaced the former round posts in portál construction. One of the most practical innovations was in roof treatment. Kiln-fired brick was used to cap the exposed parapet walls of flat-roofed buildings, especially in Santa Fe, while in the mountain communities and elsewhere pitched roofs frequently replaced the flat leak-prone ones.

Territorial architecture was the major style until after the coming of the railroad in 1879 and continued in many of the more isolated northern communities until very recently.

The increasing number of people who poured into New Mexico from eastern and midwestern areas, and some from foreign countries, in the 1870's and 1880's built their homes and commercial structures in the style with which they were familiar, even though some of the latter were no longer fashionable elsewhere. Many fine Victorian buildings of this period are still standing. Early residents of Silver City constructed handsome two-story residences of locally fired brick. Other structures include the stone U.S. Courthouse in Santa Fe, the Ilfeld Building in Las Vegas and the palatial Queen Anne-style Montezuma Hotel built at a hot springs area near Las Vegas to serve tourists arriving on the Santa Fe Railroad. The pretentious residences of some affluent political leaders of the decade still survive, especially the French Academic, three-story, 32-room mansarded home of M. W. Mills in Springer and the ornate log-sandstone ranch house of Arkansas Senator and land speculator Stephen W. Dorsey at Chico Springs.

As the period progressed, however, other architectural materials and developments were used, such as business blocks with pressed iron fronts and square stores of red brick or artificial stone equipped with large plate glass windows. The new towns which sprang up largely because of the expansion of the railroads and mining industry were laid out in the typical gridiron street pattern with little to distinguish them from urban areas in the rest of the country. Even the railroads contributed to the variety of styles with the AT&SF adopting a combination of California mission and New Mexico Spanish-Pueblo revival features.

In the early 1900's a reaction to the loss of New Mexico's unique indigenous architectural heritage due to these importations resulted in a revival of the Spanish-Pueblo-Territorial style in Taos, Albuquerque and especially in Santa Fe. This movement which reached its height in the 1930's resulted in the construction of many fine public buildings and charming homes in newer urban areas which were laid out in the historical narrow, winding street pattern. Attempts since World War II to adapt these characteristics to commercial and public buildings as well as to rapidly constructed residential developments have, however, resulted in the loss of much of their vitality and integrity.

From 1850 to statehood in 1912 the legislature, consisting of the House of Representatives and an upper body known as the Council, was elected by the people to pass laws governing the Territory of New Mexico. A congressional delegate was also selected every two years. Elections to this position were often hotly contested but many able delegates represented the region on the floor of Congress although they could not vote even on issues directly concerning their constituents. Territorial administrations generally reflected the philosophy and policies of the dominant political party in control of Washington since the governors and other major office-holders were appointed by the President of the United States. Because of the opportunities which largely developed rapidly with the opening up of the territory after the Civil War, especially in land speculation, an interlocking clique of enterprising attorneys, businessmen, large ranchers and promoters virtually controlled the economic and political life of the territory. "The Santa Fe Ring," as it was called, was affiliated with both major political parties and often acted in alliance with territorial and federal office-holders.

Miguel A. Otero was inaugurated as governor in 1897, the only Hispano to be appointed to that position, and served until 1906 thus holding the longest term of any New Mexico chief executive. When the Spanish-American War broke out in 1898, his enthusiastic response to President McKinley's call for volunteers to serve under Col. Leonard Wood and Lt. Col. Theodore Roosevelt resulted in New Mexico's quota of "Rough Riders" being raised within a few days. Much railroad construction, the establishment of new towns in the eastern portion of the territory, the building of irrigation systems and rapid increases in population took place during Otero's administration.

Throughout the long territorial period until 1912, the people of New Mexico labored in vain for statehood. Attempts in 1850, 1867 and during the 1870's failed completely. A constitution was drawn up in 1889 but was decisively defeated by the voters. Joint statehood for Arizona and New Mexico was attempted in 1906 but was rejected in Arizona. However, the Enabling Act passed by Congress in 1910 resulted in the calling of a constitutional convention which drafted the constitution ratified by the voters in January 1911. On January 6, 1912 President William Howard

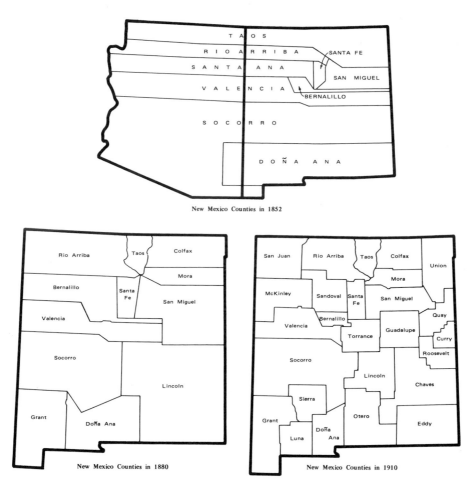

New Mexico Counties in 1852

New Mexico Counties in 1880

New Mexico Counties in 1910

New Mexico County Boundaries
Charles F. Coan

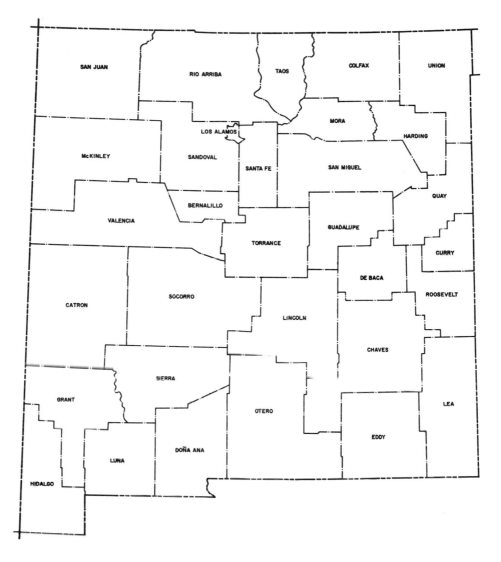

New Mexico, 1974

Taft signed the bill admitting New Mexico as the 47th state of the Union. Unlike the constitutions of most western states, the New Mexico document was extremely conservative and had no provisions for such direct democratic measures as the initiative, recall or women's suffrage. Not until the adoption of the 19th Amendment to the federal constitution in 1920 did women have the right to vote. On the other hand, the voting and educational rights of Spanish-speaking citizens were protected by equal recognition of both languages and denial of separate schools. Indians received the right to vote in 1948 after a district court decision struck down, constitutional barriers and since then the Navajos, particularly, have taken an active role in political affairs. In 1969 a constitutional convention drafted a new constitution to replace the much-amended 1910 document, but the proposal was defeated by the voters.

William C. McDonald, the first state governor, served from 1912 to January 1917. During his administration, Mexican revolutionaries of Francisco Villa's band raided the town of Columbus on March 9, 1916 killing several soldiers and civilians. A military expedition under Brigadier-General John J. Pershing pursued the raiders into Mexico but failed to capture Villa. A clash with the Mexican troops at Parral, on April 12, resulted in such a tense diplomatic situation that the troops were withdrawn by the United States government.

During World War I the legislature created the State Council of Defense to mobilize the state's resources, and more than 17,000 men saw active service in that great conflict. Problems of post-war readjustment, drought and falling prices marked the period of 1919–1924 but economic problems were somewhat lessened by the discoveries of gas and oil in northwestern San Juan County and in the southeastern Permian Basin. Together with the rest of the nation, New Mexico experienced a period of temporary prosperity beginning in 1925 which was abruptly ended by the Great Depression of 1929. The various New Deal policies for recovery were vigorously pushed in the state, especially during the 1935–1938 administrations of Governor Clyde Tingley.

New Mexico suffered the highest casualty rate of any state after the Japanese attack on Pearl Harbor, December 7, 1941 plunged the nation into World War II. The 200th and 515th Coast Artillery Anti-aircraft Regiments stationed in the Philippines were finally overwhelmed when the Bataan peninsula fell to the Japanese in

April 1942. Those who survived this attack and the ensuing "Bataan Death March" suffered three years of prison camp internment. The state furnished more than its share of servicemen in other theaters of the conflict also, as descendants of the first Spanish settlers fought side by side with descendants of the Navajo, Apache and Pueblo Indians whom they had conquered, as well as the descendants of the Anglos who had occupied New Mexico and late newcomers.

Meanwhile, New Mexico was assuming an even more important role by producing the atomic bombs which were dropped on Hiroshima and Nagasaki hastening the end of the war and ushering in the nuclear age. In 1943 the Los Alamos Ranch School on the Pajarito Plateau of the Jémez Mountains was taken over by the U.S. government to house the scientists involved in the secret Manhattan Project. The first atomic bomb, produced at Los Alamos, was tested at Trinity Site in White Sands, July 16, 1945.

Sparked by the Atomic Energy Laboratory at Los Alamos, New Mexico has continued to be. the leading region in the development of nuclear energy for peaceful as well as for military purposes. The "Gas Buggy" and "Nome" projects for underground utilization of atomic energy hold promise for industrial use and the Meson facility at Los Alamos is particularly involved in medical research.

Recent years have witnessed concentration upon water and conservation programs, with the completion of the Jémez Dam in 1953 and San Marcial Channelization Project in 1959, the construction of Navajo Dam on the San Juan River as the first phase of the Colorado River Storage Project in 1962, the Abiquiu Dam in 1963 and the current Cochiti Dam program. The State Engineer's office has conducted a systematic program of adjudicating water rights along the tributaries of the Rio Grande during the past several years. Much progress has also been made in such areas as increased support for public education at all levels, professionalization of state agencies and institutions and modernization of the court system.

New Mexico's rich history, its people, scenery and artistic contributions have long combined to form an attraction for the visitor which has developed into the state's major industry of tourism.

SELECTED BIBLIOGRAPHY

Adams, Eleanor B., *Bishop Tamaron's Visitation of New Mexico,* 1954.

Adams, Eleanor B. and Fray Angelico Chavez, *The Missions of New Mexico, 1776,* 1956.

Arrowsmith, Rex, *Mines of the Old Southwest,* 1963.

Baldwin, Gordon C., *The Warrior Apaches,* 1965.

Beck, Warren, *Historical Atlas of New Mexico,* 1969.

Bolton, Herbert Eugene, *Coronado on the Turquoise Trail, Knight of Pueblos and Plains,* reprint, 1964.

Bolton, Herbert Eugene, *Pageant in the Wilderness,* 1950.

Boyd, E., *Popular Arts of Spanish New Mexico,* 1974.

C. de Baca, Fabiola, *We Fed Them Cactus,* 1954.

Chavez, Fray Angélico, *Origins of New Mexico Families,* 1951.

Christiansen, Paige W. and Frank E. Kottlowski, eds., *New Mexico, A Mosaic of Science and History,* 1963.

Cleland, Robert Glass, *This Reckless Breed of Men,* 1950.

Colton, Ray C., *The Civil War in the Western Territories,* 1959.

Dickey, Roland, *New Mexico Village Arts,* 1949.

Dozier, Edward P., *The Pueblo Indian of North America,* 1970.

Dutton, Bertha P., *Indians of New Mexico,* 1973.

Ellis, Richard N., ed., *New Mexico Past and Present, a Historical Reader,* 1971.

Espinosa, Gilberto and Tibo J. Chavez, *El Rio Abajo,* 1966.

Espinosa, J. Manuel, *Crusaders of the Rio Grande,* 1942.

Fitzpatrick, George, *This is New Mexico,* 1948.

Fitzpatrick, George and John L. Sinclair, *Profile of a State, New Mexico,* 1964.

Frazer, Robert W., *Forts of the West,* 1965.

French, William, *Some Recollections of a Western Ranchman,* 2nd edition, 1965.

Gilbert, Jim, ed., *The Arts in New Mexico,* State Planning Office, 1966.

González, Nancie L., *The Spanish-Americans of New Mexico, a Heritage of Pride,* 2nd edition, 1969.

Hackett, Charles W., *Revolt of the Pueblo Indians of New Mexico 1680–1682*, 2 vols., 2nd edition, 1970.

Hammond, George P. and Agapito Rey, *Don Juan de Oñate*, 2 vols., 1953.

Hammond, George P. and Agapito Rey, *The Rediscovery of New Mexico, 1580–1594*, 1966.

Hester, James J., *Early Navajo Migrations and Acculturations in the Southwest,* 1962.

Hewett, Edgar L., *The Chaco Canyon and its Monuments,* 1936.

Hewett, Edgar L., *Pajarito Plateau and its Ancient People,* 1938.

Holmes, Jack E., *Politics in New Mexico,* 1967.

Horn, Calvin, *New Mexico's Troubled Years,* 1963.

Jaramillo, Cleofas M., *Shadows of the Past,* reprint, 1972.

Jenkins, Myra Ellen, *Guide to the Mexican Archives of New Mexico,* 1969.

Jenkins, Myra Ellen, *Guide to the Spanish Archives of New Mexico,* 1967.

Keleher, William A., *Turmoil in New Mexico, 1846–1868,* 1952.

Kelly, Daniel T., *The Buffalo Head,* 1972.

Kenner, Charles L., *A History of New Mexican-Plains Indian Relations,* 1969.

Lavender, David, *Bent's Fort,* 1954.

Larson, Robert L., *New Mexico's Quest for Statehood, 1846–1912,* 1968.

Mann, E. B. and Fred E. Harvey, *New Mexico, Land of Enchantment,* 1955.

McGregor, John C., *Southwestern Archeology,* 1965.

McNitt, Frank, *Navajo Wars,* 1972.

Meinig, D. W., *The Southwest: Three People in Geographic Change, 1600–1970.* 1971.

Moorhead, Max L., *The Apache Frontier,* 1968.

Moorhead, Max L., *New Mexico's Royal Road,* 1958.

Myrick, David F., *New Mexico's Railroads, an Historical Survey,* 1970.

Pearce, T. M., ed., *New Mexico Place Names,* 1968.

Reeve, Frank D., *New Mexico, a Short, Illustrated History,* 1964.

Rittenhouse, Jack D., *The Santa Fe Trail, a Historical Bibliography,* 1971.

Schroeder, Albert H., ed., *The Changing Ways of Southwestern Indians,* 1973.

Schroeder, Albert H. and Don Matson, *A Colony on the Move, Gaspar Castaño de Sosa's Journal, 1590–1591,* 1965.

Scholes, France V., *Church and State in New Mexico 1610–1650,* 1937.

Scholes, France V., *Troublous Times in New Mexico 1659–1670,* 1942.

Simmons, Marc, *The Little Lion of the Southwest,* 1974.

Simmons, Marc, *Spanish Government in New Mexico,* 1968.

Smith, Anne M., *New Mexico Indians,* 1966.

Stark, Richard B., *Music of the Spanish Folk Plays in New Mexico,* 1969.

Taylor, Morris F., *First Mail West, Stagecoach Lines on the Santa Fe Trail,* 1971.

Thomas, A. B., *After Coronado,* 1966.

Trimmer, Maurice, *The Story of New Mexico,* 1974.

Twitchell, Ralph Emerson, *Leading Facts in New Mexican History,* 2 vols., reprint, 1963.

U.S. Department of the Interior, National Park Service, *The Santa Fe Trail,* 1963.

Underhill, Ruth M., *The Navajos,* 1958.

Weber, David J., *The Taos Trappers, The Fur Trade in the Far Southwest 1540–1846,* 1971.

Weigle, Marta, *The Penitentes of the Southwest,* 1970.

Westphall, Victor, *The Public Domain in New Mexico,* 1965.

Wormington, H. M., *Prehistoric Indians of the Southwest,* 1973.

INDEX

of entry, 44; U.S.-Mexico war, 44, 49; retreat of Armijo, 44; surrender of New Mexico, 44; 1847 uprising, 49; choice of citizenship, 50; foreign capital into, 56, 63–66; separation from Mexican Diocese, 66; archdiocese, 67; arts and crafts, 70–71; statehood, 73, 76. *See also* Architecture; Arts and crafts; Civil War; Education; Mexican Period; Pueblo Indians and other tribal names; Railroads; Ranching; Religion; Treaty of Guadalupe Hidalgo; Territory of New Mexico

New Mexico Art League (Albuquerque): 71

Nome. *See* Science

Nueva Galicia, Mexico: 14

Office of Surveyor-General: 61

Ohke (San Juan Pueblo): 19

Oil: 63, 76

Ojo del Gallo: 51

Ojo del Oso. *See* Bear Springs

Oñate. *See* Juan de Oñate

Organic Law of the Territory (Kearny Code): 47

Original Inhabitants: 1–11

Ortiz, Juan Felipe (vicar): 37

Ortiz Mountains: 41, 62

Otermín. *See* Antonio de Otermín

Otero, Miguel A. (governor): 73

Otero Family: 63

Our Lady of Guadalupe (mission): 22

Our Lady of Light (chapel); 67

Our Lady of the Assumption (image): 22–23

Pacific Coast: 2, 30

Pajarito Plateau: 10, 77

Palace of the Governors: vi, 20, 22, 33, 44, 47

Parral, Chihuahua (Mexico): 76

Pawnee Indians: 30

Pearl Harbor, Hawaii: 76

Pecos Irrigation Project: 56

Pecos Pueblo (National Monument): 5, 14, 17, 24, 37

Pecos River: 17, 36, 51, 55–56, 65

Pedro de Peralta (governor): 20

Pedro de Tovar (exploration): 14

Penitentes. *See* Religion

Peralta: 51

Pérez, Albino (governor): 34, 41–42, 44

Permian Basin: 63, 76

Pershing, John J. (brig. gen.): 76

Petríz de Cruzate, Domingo Jironza (governor): 22

Phelps-Dodge Corporation: 66

Philippines: 76

Phillips, Bert G. (artist): 71

Picuris Pueblo: 17, 24

Pike, Zebulon (exploration): 30

Pino, Pedro Bautista (delegate to Spain): 31

Pinos Altos: 55, 61

Piro Pueblos: 7, 10, 20, 22, 24. *See also* names of individual pueblos

Pit House. *see* Architecture

Plains Indians: 7, 14, 17

Plan of Tomé: 42

Political affairs: 73, 76. *See also* Mexican Period; New Mexico: civil affairs; Spaniards; United States

Polk, James K. (president): 44, 47

Popé (San Juan Indian, Pueblo Revolt): 22

Pottery: 2, 7, 10, 70

Presbyterian. *See* Religion

Price, Sterling (colonel): 49

Printing: 40

Protestant: 68, 70

Provincias Internas: 19, 34

Puaray Pueblo: 17, 24

Pueblo Colorado Ruin: 7

Pueblo Indians. villages, vi; revolt, vi, 10, 22–24 supplies confiscated, 15, 17, 20; territory shrinkage, 19–20, 24; Spanish trespassers, 20, 23; relocation of, 23–24; as auxiliary forces, 26, 77; way of life, 24, 26, 30, 37, 66; lands, 23, 37, 47, 57, 61; delegation to Santa Fe, 47; citizenship, 37, 61. *See also* crafts; Epidemics; names of individual pueblos; names of linguistic groups

Pueblo Lands Board: 61

Pueblo Revolt. *See* Pueblo Indians

Puyé Ruin: 10

Pyramid Mountains: 62

Quarai (State Monument): 20

Queen Anne Style. *See* Architecture

Quivira (Kansas): 14, 17

Railroads: Atchison, Topeka, and Santa Fe, 64–65, 72; Denver and Rio Grande Western, 64–65; Southern Pacific, 64; Atlantic and Pacific, 64; Chili Line, 64–65; Texas, Santa Fe, and Northern 65; Colorado and Southern, 65; El Paso and Northeastern, 65; Chicago, Rock Island, and Pacific, 66; Dawson Railway, 66; El Paso and Southwestern, 66; mentioned, 56, 64, 72

Ralston (later Shakespeare): 62

Ramah: 70

Ranching: 20, 23, 55–56, 61

Ranchos de Taos: 42

Raton: 62

Raton Pass: 34, 36, 64

Recopilación de Leyes de los Reynos de las Indias: 23

Reed, Hiram W. (Baptist missionary): 67

Taos (Don Fernando de): 37, 49, 67, 71–72
Taos Fair: 30
Taos Pueblo: 7, 10, 14, 17, 20, 22, 26, 49
Taos Society of Artists: 71
Territorial Style. *See* Architecture
Territory of New Mexico: 50, 57, 61, 73
Tewa Pueblos: 7, 24. *See also* names of individual pueblos
Texas: 13, 24, 42, 50, 55, 65
Texas, Santa Fe, and Northern. *See* Railroads
Three Rivers Petroglyph and Pueblo Site: 5
Tiguex: 15, 17
Tingley, Clyde (governor): 76
Tiwa Pueblos: 7, 14, 17, 22, 24. *See also* names of individual pueblos
Tomé: 26
Tompiro Pueblos: 7, 10, 20. *See also* names of individual pueblos
Towa Pueblos: 7. *See also* names of individual pueblos
Trade: prehistoric, 2, 7; historic period mention, 24, 26, 30, 36, 49, 63; plains, 29–30; comanchero, 30; barriers, 31, 34; foreign, 34–37, 40. *See also* Camino Real; Chihuahua; Mountain Men; Santa Fe-Chihuahua Trail; Santa Fe Trail; Spanish Trail
Transportation. *See* Railroads; Stage lines
Treaty of Cordova, Mexico: 33, 37
Treaty of Guadalupe Hidalgo: 49, 57
Trinidad, Colorado: 64
Trinity Site. *See* Science
Tsiping (ruin): 5
Tucumcari: 66
Tuerto Mountains: 41, 62
Tularosa Basin: 65
Tully, Pinkney R. (trader): 71
Turley, Simeon (trader): 49
Two Grey Hills Archeological District: 5

United States: Louisiana Purchase 30; campaigns, 30, 51, 55; war with Mexico, 44, 49; surrender of New Mexico, 33, 44; U.S. Territory, 23, 47, 63; Treaty of Guadalupe Hidalgo, 50; citizenship, 49–50, 61; Gadsden Purchase, 50; Civil War, 50, 57; land ownership, 23, 57; New Deal, 76; Spanish-American War, 73; World War I, 76; World War II, 72, 76–77; war with Mexico, 76; mentioned, 40, 56, 62. *See also* forts by name
United States Courthouse (Santa Fe): 72
U.S. Indian Claim Commission: 61
University of New Mexico: 70
Utah: 30, 70
Utes: 11, 24, 26, 30, 37, 41

Vargas. *See* Diego de Vargas
Vasques de Coronado, Francisco (expedition): 14, 17
Vélez de Escalante, Sylvestre (Franciscan): 29
Vera Cruz Squadron: 42, 44
Vermejo River: 66
Vial, Pedro (explorer): 30
Victoria, Guadalupe (Mexican president): 33
Victorian Style. *See* Architecture
Vigil, Donanciano (acting governor): 49
Vigil y Alaríd, Juan Bautista (acting governor): 44
Villa, Francisco (Mexican revolutionary): 76
Villagrá, Gaspar Pérez de (poet-soldier): 19
Visitations. *See* Missions

Wallace, Lewis (governor): 56
Washington D.C.: 73
Watrous (formerly La Junta): 70
Western Expansion: 47, 50, 55
Westport, Missouri: 36
White Mountains: 55
White Oaks: 62, 66
White Sands: 77
Wood, Leonard (colonel): 73
Woodrow Ruin: 2
World War. *See* United States

Yellow House (ruin): 7
Yuqueyunque Pueblo: 19, 24

Zacatecas, Mexico: 19
Zia Pueblo: 24
Zuni Mountains: 50
Zuni Pueblos: 7, 13–14, 17, 20, 24, 26, 29